MEXICAN
L I G H T
—COOKING—

MEXICAN
L I G H T
──COOKING──

By Kathi Long

A JOHN BOSWELL ASSOCIATES/KING HILL PRODUCTIONS BOOK

A PERIGEE BOOK

Perigee Books
are published by
The Putnam Publishing Group
200 Madison Avenue
New York, NY 10016

Library of Congress Cataloging-in-Publication Data

Long, Kathi
  Mexican light cooking / Kathi Long.
    p. cm.
  Includes index.
  ISBN 0-399-51741-3 (trade pbk.)
  1. Cookery, Mexican. I. Title.
TX716.M4L56 1992   91-38247
641.5972—dc20   CIP

Design by Nan Jernigan/The Colman Press
Cover illustration and design by Richard Rossiter
Printed in the United States of America

1 2 3 4 5 6 7 8 9 10

This book is printed on acid-free paper.

To Barbara Kafka, who gave me the invaluable gift of her knowledge and expertise.

To Brendan Walsh, who gave me the opportunity to work with the best.

And to Patricia Quintana, who never ceases to amaze me.

CONTENTS

Slim Guacamole, Party Nachos and Spicy Pinto Bean Dip are just a few of the tasty starters and party food you'll find here. Also included are an assortment of salsas and condiments that add extra zest to the Mexican table.

For starters or to make a meal, choose from the light—Roasted Garlic Soup, Herbed Shrimp Soup, Tomato Soup with Green Chiles and Egg Noodles—and the low-calorie but hearty—Creamy Corn Soup, Black Bean Soup, Mexican Vegetable Chowder.

Here are all your favorites you thought you couldn't afford on a diet: tacos, tostadas, burritos, fajitas and casseroles, "Roll Your Own" Chicken and Vegetable Tacos, Spicy Beef Fajitas, Mushroom Quesadillas with Chipotle Tomato Sauce and Enchiladas Suizas Casserole are just a sampling.

Introduction

Ask any group of people who love Mexican cooking to name their favorite dishes, and chances are you'll hear a familiar chorus: nachos, tacos, fajitas, burritos, guacamole. Clearly we Americans have fallen in love with the zesty flavors, rib-sticking satisfaction and mouth-watering piquancy of these snack-like dishes, which are typical of "Tex-Mex," "Cal-Mex" and Southwestern American cooking in general. But there's a lot more to Mexican food than meets the North American eye. Of course, Mexicans eat tacos, just the same way we eat a chicken salad sandwich or a sliced turkey club, often using leftover meat and usually loaded with lettuce, onions, fresh chiles and other condiments. But on my travels throughout Mexico, I've discovered that their cuisine also encompasses plenty of more sophisticated but less starchy dishes, which feature seafood, chicken and fresh vegetables. Red Snapper Veracruzana, with tomatoes, olives and capers, Chiles Stuffed with Corn and Zucchini and Mexican Chicken Soup with Crispy Tortilla Strips and Lime are typical examples.

The spirited flavor of Mexican cooking makes it perfect for slimming down. Markets in Mexico City are piled high with small mountains of colorful produce of all description, trucked in daily from the surrounding countryside. Fresh fish like red snapper, pompano and tuna, scallops, shrimp and squid, flown in daily from the coasts, glisten on display. Fresh limes, chiles, ripe tomatoes, corn, avocados, mangoes, turkeys, chickens all add to the blend of indigenous Mexican cooking, based largely on tortillas, chiles, corn, rice and beans, with the Spanish influence that came later, clearly preserved in dishes like Paella and Gazpacho. This book offers light versions of both, as well as many nutritious recipes I developed, which incorporate the flavors of Mexico with the foods most readily found north of the border: Grilled Flank Steak with Black and White Chili Beans, Quesadillas with Roasted Peppers, Onions and Garlic, Lamb Fajitas with Cucumber Relish.

In *Mexican Light Cooking,* I've amplified the naturally lean aspects of the food and reduced the fat—and the calories—where conventional cooking might have been too heavy handed. With these recipes, calorie counters can enjoy all their favorites: nachos dripping with cheese, tacos heaped with filling and all the trimmings, chicken and beef fajitas. I've even included an extra-slim version of guacamole. Readers can also explore some of the less common, but no less tantalizing dishes: Pork Loin in Red Chile Sauce with Pineapple and Peaches and Chilled Cantaloupe Soup with Mint and Jalapeño Peppers.

To reduce fat, I've made some simple changes in technique. For example, in Mexico tortillas are traditionally fried in generous amounts of lard, which is also used to "fry" sauces to develop extra flavor. Since all fats have the same high calorie count—120 calories per tablespoon—I've reduced the fat to a minimum throughout. Tortillas that need softening are simply heated in the oven. For tostadas and the like, I simply coat the tortillas lightly with vegetable cooking spray and bake them until golden and crisp.

With a large nonstick skillet—a must for anyone trying to eat lighter and consume fewer calories—the cooking spray or a single tablespoon of oil is plenty for almost any dish. And where a little fat *is* needed, I've lightened the recipe even further by substituting olive oil for the lard. Besides feeling lighter on the tongue, olive oil has no cholesterol, and it is largely monosaturated, which some studies have shown has a tendency to help lower bad cholesterol in the blood. Another reason I chose olive oil is because, like lard, it is flavorful, and it is hardly an unknown quantity in Mexico. Spanish settlers introduced it centuries ago. Of course, corn oil is even more plentiful there, and if you prefer, you can substitute that or any other vegetable oil of your choice.

Recipes have also been lightened by replacing heavier, calorie-laden ingredients with lean alternatives wherever possible and by increasing the amounts of healthy vegetables in a dish. Chicken broth is used in place of oil and cream. Egg whites replace whole eggs where possible. Low-fat yogurt and reduced-calorie, no-cholesterol mayonnaise take the place of the heavy cultured cream favored in Mexico. Reduced-fat cheeses and naturally low-calorie foods, like tomatoes, peppers, chicken and seafood, which are an intrinsic part of Mexican cooking, allow tremendous variety with no sacrifice of flavor.

Throughout *Mexican Light Cooking* I've kept the availability of ingredients in mind. While Mexicans utilize a dizzying variety of chiles of all colors, sizes and descriptions, ranging from rich and mellow to fiery hot, I've restricted myself to the few that are most commonly seen in supermarkets across the country (see *About the Ingredients*, p. 13). Where recipes do call for the hotter chiles—chipotle peppers in adobo sauce, pickled jalapeño peppers or crushed hot red peppers—I've given the amounts I feel are most appropriate for the dish. If you or anyone else in your family prefers milder food, just reduce the amount of hot pepper. A certain dish may be more authentically Mexican when highly spiced, but your dining pleasure should always be the first consideration.

Many of the ingredients used in Mexican cooking are largely the same as those used north of the border. However, the numerous dried chiles and several of the herbs and exotic vegetables are hard to come by. To make this book as accessible as possible, I purposely developed the recipes using, by and large, only those ingredients I felt were reasonably available in supermarkets in many cities across the country. In a few instances, where I felt it necessary to include a food that might be difficult to find, I included a more common substitution.

About the Calorie Counts: All calories are rounded off to the nearest whole number. When a sauce is added to or placed on a dish, that amount is included in the count of the main recipe. If it is passed or served alongside as accompaniment, the calorie count is separate.

About the Ingredients

Below are tips on using some well-known ingredients and more detailed information about the Mexican foods you may not be as familiar with.

AVOCADOS—Look for the dark green, pebbly-skinned avocados, which are creamier and have a richer flavor than the smooth-skinned variety. When at their peak, they are almost black and as soft as ripe peaches. If necessary, buy them a couple of days in advance and let them stand at room temperature until they are fully ripened.

CHAYOTE—This small, mild-flavored, pale green squash, sometimes called "vegetable pear," is becoming more common in supermarkets and at green-grocers, though, of course, it is most readily found in Latin American food shops. The prickly skinned variety should be peeled before use. Chayote is good steamed, baked and stir-fried and, while its texture is crisper and firmer, its taste resembles zucchini, which is suggested as a substitute.

CHEESES—Many cheeses we know are now produced in Mexico, but not all their traditional varieties are found here. Throughout the book, I've suggested the North American cheese that has the closest character to the type that would be used there. Reduced-fat cheeses are always called for; they cut saturated fat and can reduce calories by 50 percent or more.

CHILES—*Chile* is the generic Mexican word for any of a large number of capsicum peppers, which range from mild to fiery hot. In this country, the word used by itself refers to the most common ordinary fresh chile, or hot pepper, which may be red or green. Often seen in supermarkets and green-grocers, it is narrow, rather corkscrew shaped and anywhere from 2 to 4 inches in length. Roasted and peeled green chiles, whole and diced, are commonly sold in supermarkets in 4-ounce cans. A larger roasted chile, appropriate for stuffing, is sold in a 27-ounce can. The word *chili* in this book refers to the powder that includes not only ground red chile peppers, but also added spices and is sold as chili powder or chili con carne in major spice lines. For descriptions of some of the specialized types of chiles, such as jalapeños and chipotles, see PEPPERS.

CILANTRO—This pungent herb provides one of the characteristic flavors of Mexican cookery. In fact, it is an incredibly favored herb in many cuisines throughout the world and is known also as fresh coriander (the herb is the leaf of the coriander plant) and as Chinese parsley. Accordingly, if you cannot find it in your supermarket and there is no Latin American grocery near you, you might try an Asian market, if that is more accessible. Store cilantro in the refrigerator with the stems in a glass of water and the leaves loosely covered with a plastic bag. Chop the herb just before using, because its distinctive flavor and aroma dissipate relatively quickly once it is cut. Italian flat-leaf parsley is used as a substitute for cilantro in this book. It will give you the color and some herbal quality, but the flavor will not be as authentic as cilantro's is.

JICAMA—Dark brown on the outside and turnip shaped, jicama is a large root, often weighing a pound or more. Peeled, it reveals a delicate, crisp white vegetable, with a very mild flavor and just a hint of sweetness, much like fresh water chestnuts or Jerusalem artichokes, which are eaten raw in salads. Shredded, it provides tremendous volume for very few calories.

OREGANO—The name *oregano* is applied to several herbs that are very similar in taste. Most Mexican oregano comes from a plant of the verbena family, and it is more intensely flavored than Mediterranean oregano, which is a kind of mint. At least one major spice company packages Mexican oregano in its supermarket line. Look for it also in the Mexican or ethnic food section of your store, as well as in spice shops and Latin American markets. Ordinary oregano is such a close approximation, though, that I haven't specified Mexican oregano in the recipes; if you can get it, use it.

PEPPERS—While the Mexicans use a bewildering array of assorted chile peppers, I have restricted myself to the few that are widely available and a couple without which it is almost impossible to cook Mexican food. In addition to those noted under CHILES, they are:

Anchos are mild, dried brick-red peppers that measure about 4 inches long and 2½ inches wide near the top. Some supermarkets carry anchos in plastic bags. If yours doesn't and you're planning to do a lot of Mexican cooking, it really pays to buy in quantity by mail; check food magazines for ads. Stored in tightly sealed plastic bags in the freezer, anchos will keep almost indefinitely. The closest substitute to an ancho would be a New Mexican chile, which is only slightly hotter. Where ground ancho powder is called for, a mild ground red chile powder, available in spice stores or by mail order, can be used instead.

Chipotles are dried, smoked jalapeños, and they are fiery hot. In Mexico they are sold dried and pickled; here they are most commonly seen canned in adobo sauce, which is the form in which I've called for them in the following recipes.

Jalapeños are small, chubby fresh green chiles with a smooth skin and rounded blunt end. They range from fairly mild to rather hot. It's really impossible to know from one batch to another without tasting, which is what I recommend you do before adding them, with due caution, of course; adjust amounts accordingly to your taste. Seeding the jalapeños and removing their whitish inner "ribs" will reduce the heat. Generic fresh green chiles can be substituted for jalapeños, though the flavor will not be quite the same.

Pickled jalapeño peppers, probably most reknowned for topping off nachos, are available in practically every supermarket, both whole and sliced. I've used them and their pickling juice a lot in these recipes to give a Mexican flavor with an ingredient I know everyone can get. They are usually sold labeled as mild, medium and hot. I use medium; choose your favorite and adjust the amounts called for in the recipes as necessary.

PUMPKIN SEEDS—Also called *pepitas,* these are hulled, raw unsalted pumpkin seeds that are often used toasted and ground to thicken Mexican sauces. They go all the way back to the Aztecs, but you can find them at your local health food store. Store in the freezer in a tightly closed container, as you would any nut.

TOMATILLOS—These small Mexican green tomatoes with their papery outer husks are not unripened red tomatoes, but a close relative of the ground cherry, which grows wild throughout much of the United States. The unique tart flavor of tomatillos forms the basis of most green sauces and is an intrinsic element in Mexican cooking. While fresh tomatillos are beginning to turn up in produce departments in many more areas of the country, I have called for canned ones since that seems to be the more common form available. If you can get fresh tomatillos, remove the papery husks and boil them before using for about 10 minutes in a large saucepan of water until tender.

TORTILLAS—While the aroma of fresh-baked tortillas perfumes the air in every Mexican city and village, most of us must settle for packaged brands. The good news is that prepared tortillas are now found in supermarkets across the country, usually in the refrigerated section and sometimes frozen. While corn tortillas are standardly 6 to 7 inches in diameter, flour tortillas come in a wider assortment of sizes. In this book, all tortillas are assumed to be 6 to 7 inches in diameter. A few recipes call for prepared taco shells. These are precooked, dried and boxed, and they can be found in the Mexican food section of most supermarkets.

Chapter One

PARTY FOOD
AND
SNACKS

When it comes to entertaining for company or snacking in front of the VCR, the zesty flavors of Mexican food provide both a festive air and a wide variety from which to choose. Spicy and tantalizing on the tongue, Mexican appetizers are exceptionally enticing. Lean in fat and low in calories, these hors d'oeuvres, dips and salsas pique the appetite without being overly filling.

Salsa is literally the Spanish word for sauce, but it has come to stand for the red tomato-based sauce/condiment/dip usually set in front of you with a basket of chips the moment you enter a Mexican restaurant in this country. With the supermarket accessibility of packaged tortilla chips, often called tostadas, and bottled salsa, it's become the snack of choice for many of us at home as well.

Luckily for calorie-conscious eaters, this type of salsa is naturally light. Made without oil, depending on the recipe, salsas come in at anywhere from 11 to 15 calories a quarter-cup, a dieter's delight. The tortilla chips, however, are another matter. Commercial chips range anywhere from 140 to 150 calories an ounce. That's why I've included a make-your-own recipe for Crispy Corn Tostadas that produces 8 good-sized chips, almost 2 ounces, for only 93 calories, low enough to allow you a few extra for a party or special snack.

Besides salsas, this chapter offers zesty condiments and an assortment of other dips to serve with the tortilla chips or with a basket of fresh vegetables—an extra-lean version of guacamole, South-of-the-Border

White Bean Dip, with roasted red peppers and mild roasted green chiles, to name a couple. Besides three kinds of nachos, including Party Nachos with all the trimmings, you'll find hot hors d'oeuvres, such as Empanaditas with Spiced Ground Beef Filling and Appetizer Quesadillas, flour tortilla triangles, filled with a mix of goat cheese and Monterey Jack. Depending on the occasion and how many calories you can afford to add, look also at Chapter 3, Tortillas in All Their Glory, for more ideas for entertaining.

Red Snapper Seviche

The acid in the lime juice "cooks" the fish in this refreshing appetizer. Be sure to use only the very freshest fish.

6 SERVINGS   137 CALORIES PER SERVING

1 pound red snapper fillets (or another meaty, white-fleshed ocean fish,
*   such as sea bass, grouper or halibut)*
1 cup fresh lime juice (from 5 to 6 limes)
1 large ripe tomato, cut into ½-inch dice
1 medium red onion, cut into ¼-inch dice
1 small cucumber, peeled, seeded and cut into ¼-inch dice
1 can (4 ounces) diced roasted green chiles, drained
6 medium radishes, thinly sliced and cut into thin strips
¼ cup chopped cilantro or parsley
2 tablespoons extra virgin olive oil
½ to ¾ teaspoon salt
Sprigs of cilantro or parsley, for garnish

1. Run your fingers carefully along the midline of the fillets to see whether any bones have been left in. If there are, remove them by taking a sharp knife and cutting to one side of the bones down the length of the fillet. Then run the knife close to the bones on the other side to cut a thin strip containing the bones and discard. Cut the fish into ½-inch cubes and place in a medium glass bowl.

2. Pour the lime juice over the fish and stir several times so the pieces are not stuck together. Cover with plastic wrap and refrigerate 6 to 8 hours, or overnight, until the fish has lost its translucency and is white throughout.

3. Drain the fish thoroughly. In a medium bowl, combine the fish with the tomato, red onion, cucumber, chiles, radishes, cilantro, oil and salt. Toss gently to mix. If not using immediately, cover with plastic wrap and refrigerate until serving time. Garnish with sprigs of cilantro or parsley.

Slim Guacamole

Avocado contains no cholesterol, but its smooth, creamy consistency comes from unsaturated fat, which adds up to calories. This leaner version of the classic Mexican dip gets rid of a good deal of the fat without sacrificing flavor by stretching the avocado with reduced-fat ricotta cheese and the low-calorie tomato.

MAKES 2½ CUPS   59 CALORIES PER ¼ CUP

> *1 large ripe avocado, peeled*
> *½ cup reduced-fat ricotta cheese*
> *1 medium ripe tomato, finely diced*
> *½ medium white onion, finely diced*
> *2 tablespoons fresh lime juice*
> *3 fresh jalapeño peppers, seeded and minced, or ¼ teaspoon cayenne*
> *   pepper*
> *½ teaspoon salt*

1. In a medium bowl, mash together the avocado and ricotta cheese with a fork until the mixture is well blended but the avocado still has some texture.

2. Fold in the tomato and onion. Season the guacamole with the lime juice, jalapeño peppers and salt. If not using immediately, place a piece of plastic wrap directly on top of the guacamole, smooth to cover the exposed surface completely and refrigerate.

Spicy Pinto Bean Dip

If canned chipotle peppers in adobo sauce are not available, increase the number of pickled jalapeño peppers in the recipe to five. Serve with tostadas or raw vegetables for dipping.

MAKES ABOUT 2½ CUPS   48 CALORIES PER ¼ CUP

> *1 small head of garlic*
> *1 teaspoon olive oil*

Salt and freshly ground black pepper
1 can (16 ounces) pinto beans, rinsed and drained
3 pickled jalapeño peppers
2 canned chipotle peppers in adobo sauce plus 2 teaspoons of the sauce
½ medium white onion, minced (about ½ cup)
3 tablespoons chopped cilantro or parsley

1. Preheat the oven to 375° F. Remove any loose, papery skin from the garlic and cut the whole head crosswise in half. Season the cut sides lightly with salt and pepper and wrap the pieces in aluminum foil. Bake 40 minutes, or until the garlic is golden. Remove the foil and let the garlic stand until cool.

2. Squeeze the garlic from the skins into a food processor. Add the oil, ¼ teaspoon salt and ⅛ teaspoon black pepper, the pinto beans, jalapeño peppers, chipotles with their sauce, onion and cilantro. Pulse until mixed thoroughly.

South-of-the-Border White Bean Dip

MAKES 3 CUPS   43 CALORIES PER ¼ CUP

1 can (16 ounces) white beans, rinsed and well drained
1 tablespoon olive oil
3 garlic cloves, peeled and sliced
1 can (4 ounces) diced green chiles, drained
1 jar (4 ounces) roasted red peppers, drained and diced
⅓ cup thinly sliced scallions
½ teaspoon dried thyme
½ teaspoon salt
½ teaspoon freshly ground black pepper

1. Place the beans in a large mixing bowl. Heat the olive oil in a small skillet over medium heat. Add the garlic, green chiles, roasted red peppers, scallions and thyme. Cook until the garlic is pale golden, about 2 minutes. Pour the hot vegetables and oil into the bowl with the beans and add the salt and pepper.

2. Mash the bean mixture with two forks or a potato masher, or pulse in a food processor, until coarsely puréed. Serve at room temperature.

Homemade Salsa

Here's an easy salsa made with canned tomatoes, which is appropriate as a garnish for tacos, burritos and enchiladas or as a dip for tostadas or tortilla chips.

MAKES 3½ CUPS   13 CALORIES PER ¼ CUP

> *1 can (16 ounces) whole tomatoes in purée*
> *1 medium white onion, minced*
> *½ teaspoon minced garlic*
> *½ cup finely chopped pickled jalapeño peppers*
> *⅓ cup chopped cilantro or parsley*
> *Pinch of salt*
> *2 tablespoons fresh lime juice or juice from pickled jalapeño peppers*

1. In a food processor, pulse the tomatoes and their purée to chop the tomatoes coarsely, but do not let them become a purée. Transfer to a medium bowl and add the onion, garlic, jalapeño peppers, cilantro, salt and lime juice. Stir to blend.

2. Let the salsa stand at room temperature for at least 30 minutes to allow the flavors to mellow.

Tomatillo Salsa

This green salsa makes an interesting change from the familiar "red" salsa. It is used in Enchiladas Suizas Casserole (p. 82) and as a dip with tortilla chips.

MAKES 3½ CUPS   12 CALORIES PER ¼ CUP

> *3 jalapeño peppers, fresh or pickled*
> *2 cans (11 ounces each) tomatillos, drained*
> *1 medium white onion, coarsely cut up*

2 small garlic cloves, chopped
½ cup coarsely chopped cilantro or parsley
3 tablespoons fresh lime juice
½ teaspoon salt
Pinch of sugar

Stem, seed and chop the jalapeño peppers. Put the jalapeño peppers, tomatillos, onion, garlic and cilantro in a food processor and pulse 10 times to chop. Scrape down the sides of the bowl with a rubber scraper. Add the lime juice, salt and sugar. Pulse several more times, until the seasonings are incorporated and the jalapeños and garlic are minced. Cover the salsa and refrigerate slightly before serving.

Fresh Tomato Salsa

This is a delicious fresh tomato salsa that contains no oil, so you can indulge generously in this mild sauce as an accompaniment to meat and fish or as a low-calorie dip with tortilla chips.

MAKES ABOUT 3 CUPS   11 CALORIES PER ¼ CUP

2 large ripe tomatoes (1 pound), cut into ½-inch dice
1 medium white onion, finely chopped
¼ cup chopped cilantro or parsley
1 teaspoon dried marjoram or oregano
2 tablespoons finely diced seeded jalapeño peppers (optional)
3 tablespoons fresh lime juice or red wine vinegar
½ teaspoon salt

In a medium bowl, combine the tomatoes, onion, cilantro, marjoram, jalapeño peppers, lime juice and salt. Let stand at room temperature at least 30 minutes or up to 2 hours. Cover and refrigerate for longer storage. Let return to room temperature before serving.

Nachos

You can use store-bought tortilla chips for this recipe or any of the following nachos, but the fat and caloric content will vary with the manufacturer.

8 SERVINGS   164 CALORIES PER SERVING

8 ounces reduced-fat Cheddar, Muenster or Monterey Jack cheese
8 to 10 pickled jalapeño peppers
1 recipe Crispy Corn Tostadas (p. 28) or 48 packaged tostadas or corn
  tortilla chips (about 6 ounces)

1. Preheat the broiler. Coarsely grate or shred the cheese and set aside. Cut the pickled jalapeños into ¼-inch slices. Drain the slices on paper towels.

2. Arrange the tostadas in a single layer on a baking sheet. Place about 1 teaspoon of the grated cheese on each tostada. Broil about 4 inches from the heat until the cheese is melted, 1 to 2 minutes. Top each nacho with 1 slice of the pickled jalapeño pepper and serve at once.

Party Nachos

8 SERVINGS   189 CALORIES PER SERVING

1 cup canned pinto beans, rinsed and drained
¼ teaspoon salt
¼ teaspoon freshly ground black pepper
4 ounces reduced-fat Cheddar, Muenster or Monterey Jack cheese
9 to 10 pickled jalapeño peppers
1 recipe Crispy Corn Tostadas (p. 28) or 48 packaged tostadas or corn
  tortilla chips (about 6 ounces)
1 cup Beef Taco Filling (p. 68), warmed

1. Preheat the broiler. In a food processor, combine the pinto beans, salt and pepper. Purée until smooth. Coarsely grate or shred the cheese and set aside. Cut the pickled jalapeños into ¼-inch slices. Drain the slices on paper towels.

2. Spread 1 teaspoon of the bean paste on each tostada chip. Place 1 teaspoon of beef filling on top of the beans and sprinkle 1 teaspoon of the grated cheese on top of the filling.

3. Arrange the nachos in a single layer on a baking sheet and broil about 4 inches from the heat until the cheese is melted, 1 to 2 minutes. Top each nacho with 1 slice of the pickled jalapeño pepper and serve at once.

Shrimp Nachos

6 SERVINGS   126 CALORIES PER SERVING

½ pound medium shrimp, shelled and deveined
1 tablespoon fresh lime juice
2 teaspoons corn oil
1 small garlic clove, crushed through a press
½ recipe Crispy Corn Tostadas (p. 28) or 24 packaged tostadas or
   corn tortilla chips (about 3 ounces)
½ cup coarsely shredded reduced-fat Cheddar, Muenster or Monterey
   Jack cheese (2 ounces)
4 pickled jalapeño peppers, sliced

1. Bring a medium saucepan of water to a boil over high heat. Add the shrimp, return to a boil and cook 1 minute, or until the shrimp are pink and loosely curled. Drain into a colander.

2. While they are still warm, transfer the shrimp to a small bowl. Add the lime juice, oil and garlic; toss to coat the shrimp. Let stand at room temperature for up to 30 minutes. Cover and refrigerate if not assembling the nachos.

3. Preheat the broiler. Coarsely chop the marinated shrimp. Arrange the tostadas in a single layer on a baking sheet. Top each chip with about 1 teaspoon of the shrimp. Sprinkle the cheese on top. Broil about 4 inches from the heat until the cheese is just melted, 1 minute. Top each nacho with 1 slice of the pickled jalapeño pepper. Serve hot.

Tuna with Chiles, Capers and Olives

6 SERVINGS   140 CALORIES PER SERVING

> 1 (7-ounce) can tuna in water, drained and flaked
> 2 tablespoons olive oil
> ½ cup finely chopped onion
> ¼ cup chopped pickled jalapeño peppers
> ¼ cup chopped green olives
> ¼ cup capers, drained and rinsed
> ⅓ cup finely chopped celery
> ½ cup chopped tomato
> 2 tablespoons fresh lime juice
> 2 tablespoons juice from the pickled jalapeño peppers
> ¼ teaspoon salt
> 24 to 30 tortilla chips

In a medium bowl, combine all the ingredients except the tortilla chips and toss well to mix. Serve with the tortilla chips for dipping.

Pickled Jalapeño Peppers

This is an easy, no-cook way to always have pickled jalapeño peppers on hand as well as jalapeño vinegar, which makes a flavorful addition to soups, salad dressings and sauces. Make sure you do not buy "seasoned" rice wine vinegar, which has a slightly different, sweeter flavor.

MAKES 1 QUART   2 CALORIES PER TABLESPOON

> 1 pound fresh jalapeño peppers
> 2 bottles (16.8 ounces each) Japanese rice wine vinegar

1. Pick through the peppers and discard any with soft spots or bruises. Rinse them well and dry on paper towels. Make a slit, from stem to tip, down one side of each chile. When all the chiles have been slit, put them into two 1-quart glass jars.

2. Pour the vinegar over the peppers, dividing evenly. Let the peppers marinate in the vinegar at room temperature 6 hours, then refrigerate at least 4 days before using. The chiles and vinegar will now be ready for use in any recipe calling for pickled jalapeño peppers or the juice from pickled jalapeño peppers.

3. For future use, keep the pickled peppers in the vinegar and store in the covered jar in the refrigerator. They will keep well for up to a year.

Pickled Red Onions

The bright pink color of these pickled onions makes them as attractive to the eye as to the palate. Use them as a garnish for salads or any spicy dish. They are particularly good with tacos and tostadas.

8 SERVINGS   66 CALORIES PER SERVING

> *1 cup red wine vinegar*
> *1 cup orange juice*
> *3 tablespoons sugar*
> *⅛ teaspoon salt*
> *1 tablespoon extra virgin olive oil*
> *4 medium red onions, thinly sliced*
> *1½ teaspoons dried oregano*
> *2 bay leaves, broken into halves*

In a medium bowl, combine the vinegar, orange juice, sugar and salt. Stir until the sugar is dissolved. Whisk in the olive oil. Add the red onions, oregano and bay leaves. Toss to mix thoroughly. Cover and set aside 3 hours at room temperature, then refrigerate overnight before using. The pickled onions will keep in the refrigerator for up to 3 weeks.

Crispy Corn Tostadas

6 Servings   93 Calories per serving

8 corn tortillas (6 to 7 inches in diameter)
Vegetable cooking spray
½ to 1 teaspoon salt, to taste

1. Cut the tortillas in half and then cut each half into 3 equal triangles.

2. Preheat the oven to 375° F. Place the tortilla pieces in a bowl, spray them lightly with vegetable cooking spray, toss and spread them on a baking sheet in a single layer.

3. Bake the tostadas for 10 to 12 minutes, or until pale golden and very crisp. Remove them from the oven and season them lightly with salt and serve warm or at room temperature.

Variation

Ancho Tostadas: Place 2 tablespoons of ground ancho peppers in a paper bag with ½ to 1 teaspoon of salt and add the tostada chips warm from the oven. Shake the bag to cover the chips with the ground anchos and salt. Serve warm or at room temperature.

Appetizer Quesadillas

Low-fat and reduced-fat cheeses make it possible to enjoy these cheese-filled tortillas without guilt. While quesadillas are often served as a fork-and-knife dish as a first course or for lunch, here they are cut into bite-size triangles and served with salsa for a perfect hot party appetizer.

6 SERVINGS   194 CALORIES PER SERVING

> 6 flour tortillas (6 to 7 inches in diameter)
> 4 ounces reduced-fat goat cheese, crumbled, or reduced-fat Cheddar or Longhorn cheese, shredded (about 1 cup)
> 4 ounces reduced-fat Monterey Jack cheese, shredded (about 1 cup)
> ½ teaspoon freshly ground black pepper
> 1 cup Homemade Salsa (p. 22) or your favorite bottled salsa

1. Preheat the oven to 350° F. Spray a baking sheet with vegetable cooking spray and cover it with the tortillas in a single layer.

2. Toss the cheeses together in a small bowl and sprinkle them evenly over the tortillas. Season with the pepper. Bake 5 minutes, or until the cheeses are melted.

3. Remove the baking sheet from the oven and immediately fold the tortillas in half. Cut each folded tortilla into 3 triangles. Serve warm, with a bowl of salsa for dipping.

– *Empanaditas with Spiced Ground Beef Filling* –

Pastries are one of the hardest things to accommodate on a calorie-restricted diet. Empanadas are traditionally made with a lot of lard. I've lightened them considerably by turning the dough into an easy-to-make food processor cream cheese pastry, and miniaturized the savories. These empanaditas are perfect for a snack or hot hors d'oeuvre.

10 SERVINGS   162 CALORIES PER SERVING

> *1 cup flour*
> *1 cup cornmeal, preferably stone-ground*
> *1 teaspoon ground cumin*
> *1 teaspoon salt*
> *½ teaspoon freshly ground black pepper*
> *⅛ teaspoon cayenne pepper*
> *6 ounces light cream cheese*
> *4 to 6 tablespoons ice water*
> *½ recipe Spiced Ground Beef Filling (recipe follows)*

1. Put the flour, cornmeal, cumin, salt, black pepper and cayenne in a food processor and pulse the mixture to mix well. Add the cream cheese and process steadily until blended. The mixture will still be dry and floury. With the machine on, add the ice water, 1 tablespoon at a time, until the dough just comes together in a loose ball. Remove the dough to a flat work surface.

2. Preheat the oven to 400° F. Pat the dough into a ball and cut in half. Roll half the dough to ⅛-inch thickness between two sheets of wax paper or plastic wrap. Cut the dough into 2½-inch rounds and set aside. Do the same with the remaining dough and any scraps that you can reroll. There should be 20 rounds.

3. Fill each round with about 1 teaspoon of the ground beef filling and fold in half, bringing the edges together to form a semicircle. Seal the empanaditas by pressing the edge with the tines of a fork all the way around the curve. Arrange the empanaditas on a baking sheet and bake 20 to 25 minutes, or until firm and slightly golden. Serve hot; allow 2 empanaditas per person.

Spiced Ground Beef Filling

This is double the amount you'll need to make a single recipe of the Empanaditas, but it doesn't make sense to cook up a smaller amount. Divide the cooked filling in half and freeze the unused portion in a covered plastic container for the next time you make these tasty turnovers.

MAKES ABOUT ⅔ CUP   28 CALORIES PER TABLESPOON

Vegetable cooking spray
¼ pound ground sirloin (90% lean)
2 tablespoons minced onion
1 garlic clove, minced
2 tablespoons currants
1 tablespoon tomato paste
¼ teaspoon ground cinnamon
Pinch of ground cloves
¼ teaspoon salt
⅛ teaspoon freshly ground black pepper

1. Spray a medium nonstick skillet with vegetable cooking spray and place over medium-high heat. Crumble the ground beef into the pan, add the onion and garlic and cook, stirring with a wooden spoon to break up any lumps, until the meat is lightly browned and the onion is soft, about 5 minutes. Drain in a fine sieve to remove any fat and return the mixture to the skillet.

2. Add the currants, tomato paste, cinnamon, cloves, salt, pepper and 3 tablespoons water. Cook over medium heat, stirring often, until the mixture has thickened slightly, 6 to 8 minutes. Remove from the heat and set aside to cool before using as a filling.

Chapter Two

SAVORY SOUPS

Mexican soups are naturally lean and full of flavor. Devoid of butter and cream, chock full of chicken, seafood, vegetables and beans, they provide sustenance without being too rich. While any of the soups in this chapter could provide a lovely light beginning to a meal, some are more naturally introductions to substantial food that will follow; others are so chunky and filled with good things to eat that paired with a salad or perhaps a single taco, they could easily make a meal in themselves. What's most exciting about these heartier soups, such as Double Chicken Soup with Jalapeño Peppers and Avocado, and Hearty Pinto Bean Soup, is that each could form the basis of a lovely lunch or light supper and still keep under 200 calories. Creamy Corn Soup, made with skim milk and just a touch of cornstarch, and Herbed Shrimp Soup provide novel ways to begin a Mexican or North American–style meal.

The cold soups are intriguing and exceptionally low in calories. Gazpacho, a chilled Spanish classic that tastes like a soup and a salad combined in one, comes in at well under 100 calories per serving, and the deliciously exotic, sweet-hot combination of Chilled Cantaloupe Soup with Mint and Jalapeño Peppers contains a mere 72 calories per serving. Each is so light that it could be enjoyed as a nutritious pick-me-up any time of the day, and both would make perfect starters for a late spring or summertime meal.

In Mexico, stewing hens are more common than they are here, and chicken broth is rich and flavorful. For convenience, these recipes can be made with a good brand of reduced-sodium chicken broth with all the fat skimmed off the top. Of course, homemade unsalted stock will give you the best, most authentic results.

   If you wish to make homemade stock, here is an easy recipe: Throw about four pounds of chicken backs, necks and wings into a stockpot. If you have the carcass from a roasted chicken, use that. Add a couple of onions, each stuck with a whole clove, a few carrots, celery stalks, any bits of tomato or mushroom trimmings you may have on hand, about a teaspoon of whole black peppercorns, a bay leaf and a handful of parsley. Add cold water to cover by at least an inch and bring to a boil, skimming off the foam that rises to the top. Reduce the heat to low and simmer, uncovered, at least an hour and a half to two hours. Then strain and let cool. Refrigerate until chilled, then scrape the congealed fat off the top.

Mexican Chicken Soup with Crispy Tortilla Strips and Lime

6 Servings   190 Calories per serving

4 corn tortillas
Vegetable cooking spray
1 tablespoon corn or olive oil
1 medium white onion, chopped
1 medium red bell pepper, diced
2 garlic cloves, minced
1 can (14 ounces) Italian plum tomatoes, drained and chopped
6 cups unsalted or reduced-sodium chicken broth
1 teaspoon dried marjoram
½ teaspoon dried thyme
1 bay leaf
¾ pound skinless, boneless chicken breasts, cut crosswise into paper-thin slices (see Note)
1 tablespoon plus 1 teaspoon fresh lime juice
3 fresh jalapeño or other hot green chile peppers, seeded and finely minced (optional)
1 large lime, cut into 6 wedges

1. Preheat the oven to 350° F. Cut the tortillas in half, then crosswise into ¼-inch strips. Spray the strips lightly with vegetable cooking spray and toss. Spread the strips out on a baking sheet and bake 10 minutes, or until crisp. Set aside.

2. Heat the oil in a large saucepan. Add the onion and red pepper and cook over medium heat, stirring occasionally until softened, 5 to 7 minutes. Add the garlic and cook until softened and fragrant, 1 to 2 minutes longer. Add the tomatoes, chicken broth, marjoram, thyme and bay leaf. Bring to a boil, reduce the heat and simmer over medium-low heat 10 minutes.

3. Add the chicken slices, lime juice and jalapeños. Cook until the chicken is completely white and tender, about 3 minutes. Remove and discard the bay leaf. Serve garnished with the tortilla strips and with a wedge of lime on the side to squeeze into the soup.

NOTE *Partially freezing the chicken makes it much easier to slice thinly.*

Double Chicken Soup with Jalapeño Peppers and Avocado

6 SERVINGS   136 CALORIES PER SERVING

6 cups unsalted or reduced-sodium chicken broth
3 small chicken breast halves with bones (about 6 ounces each), skin removed
2 scallions, thinly sliced
1 small ripe avocado, cut into ¼-inch dice
2 fresh jalapeño peppers, seeded and minced, or ⅛ teaspoon cayenne pepper
1 tablespoon fresh lime juice
1 tablespoon chopped cilantro or parsley
¼ teaspoon salt

1. In a large saucepan, bring the chicken broth to a boil. Add the chicken. Bring to a simmer and cook over medium-low heat 15 to 20 minutes, until the chicken is cooked through with no trace of pink near the bone. Remove the chicken to a plate to cool. Strain the chicken broth through a fine sieve and return it to the saucepan.

2. Shred the chicken and return it to the soup. Reheat if necessary. Just before serving, add the scallions, avocado, jalapeños, lime juice, cilantro and salt. Serve hot.

Gazpacho

Practically an all-you-can-eat treat for dieters, this cool, refreshing soup is best in summer, with vegetables right out of the garden or your closest farmer's market. The low-fat yogurt topping will add 9 calories per tablespoon.

8 Servings   71 Calories per serving

> 8 medium ripe tomatoes
> 1 long green "seedless" cucumber, unpeeled, or 2 large slender ordinary
>   cucumbers, peeled and seeded
> 1 medium red onion
> 1 large red bell pepper, seeded
> 1 large yellow bell pepper, seeded
> 2 large celery ribs
> 5 fresh jalapeño peppers, seeded and minced
> 4 cups tomato juice
> 3 tablespoons fresh lime juice
> 2 tablespoons sherry vinegar or red wine vinegar
> 1½ teaspoons salt
> Low-fat plain yogurt (optional)

1. Cut the tomatoes, cucumber, red onion, red and yellow bell peppers, celery and jalapeño peppers into chunks and pulse in batches in a food processor until finely chopped. Or finely chop with a large sharp knife.

2. In a large bowl or covered container, combine the chopped vegetables with the tomato juice, lime juice, vinegar and salt. Stir to mix thoroughly. Cover and refrigerate until well chilled, at least 2 hours or up to 8 hours.

3. Serve the gazpacho ice cold, topped with a dollop of yogurt, if desired.

Spicy Shrimp and Tomato Soup

This is a light but substantial soup that could easily make a lunch if served with a nice salad. The full amount of hot red pepper produces a spicy brew indeed, so adjust the amount according to your own personal taste.

6 SERVINGS   152 CALORIES PER SERVING

1 can (16 ounces) whole tomatoes with thick tomato purée
1 medium onion, chopped
1 tablespoon olive oil
2 small garlic cloves, minced
½ pound red potatoes, scrubbed and cut into ½-inch dice
½ teaspoon ground cumin
½ teaspoon dried oregano
1 bay leaf
¼ to ½ teaspoon crushed hot red pepper, to taste
¼ teaspoon freshly ground black pepper
2 cups bottled clam juice
2 cups unsalted or reduced-sodium chicken broth
¾ pound large shrimp, shelled, deveined and cut into ½-inch pieces

1. Purée the tomatoes with their purée in a food processor or blender. Set the tomato purée aside.

2. In a large nonaluminum saucepan, cook the onion in the olive oil over medium heat until softened, about 5 minutes. Add the garlic and cook 1 minute longer. Add the potatoes, tomato purée, cumin, oregano, bay leaf, crushed hot pepper and black pepper. Stir to combine. Add the clam juice and chicken broth and bring to a boil. Reduce the heat and simmer until the potatoes are tender, 5 to 7 minutes.

3. Add the shrimp and simmer 5 minutes. Remove and discard the bay leaf. Serve hot.

Herbed Shrimp Soup

Seafood is one of a calorie counter's best friends, and this soup is so hearty and flavorful it would make a perfect light lunch.

6 SERVINGS   147 CALORIES PER SERVING

1 tablespoon olive oil
1 medium white onion, thinly sliced
1 pound ripe tomatoes, chopped
3 jalapeño peppers, fresh or pickled, seeded and minced
3 cups bottled clam juice
3 cups unsalted chicken broth or water
1 teaspoon dried marjoram or oregano
1 pound medium shrimp, shelled and deveined
1 fresh lime, cut into 6 wedges

1. Heat the oil in a large saucepan over medium heat. Add the onion and cook until softened, about 3 minutes. Add the tomatoes and jalapeño peppers and cook 3 minutes longer.

2. Add the clam juice, chicken broth and marjoram. Bring to a boil, reduce the heat and simmer 5 minutes. Add the shrimp and simmer until pink, loosely curled and opaque throughout, about 5 minutes longer.

3. To serve, divide the shrimp evenly among 6 bowls and ladle the broth and vegetables over the shrimp. Serve immediately, with a wedge of lime to squeeze into each serving.

Tomato Soup with Green Chiles and Egg Noodles

Mexican tomatoes are vine ripened and glorious. This is a variation on a popular Mexican soup that celebrates this favorite low-calorie vegetable. The noodles may seem out of place, but they are a very common item in the typical Mexican cupboard.

6 Servings   85 Calories per serving

1 can (16 ounces) whole tomatoes with thick tomato purée
1 medium onion, finely chopped
1 large garlic clove, minced
1 can (4 ounces) diced green chiles, drained
6 cups unsalted or reduced-sodium chicken broth
½ teaspoon dried oregano
½ teaspoon salt
⅛ teaspoon freshly ground black pepper
1 cup fine egg noodles
1 tablespoon chopped cilantro or fresh parsley, for garnish

1. In a food processor, pulse the tomatoes, onion, garlic and chiles until the tomatoes are chopped. Pour the tomato mixture into a large nonaluminum saucepan and place over medium heat. Add the chicken broth, oregano, salt and pepper and bring to a boil.

2. Stir in the noodles and boil gently until they have softened, about 5 minutes. Garnish the soup with chopped cilantro and serve.

Roasted Garlic Soup

Garlic and onions provide wonderfully satisfying flavor without any fat. Don't be frightened by the generous amount of garlic in this soup. The long roasting and simmering softens and sweetens the flavor. This is the kind of soup you can get addicted to, and at just over 100 calories a bowl, you can afford to indulge whenever you wish.

6 SERVINGS   108 CALORIES PER SERVING

> 2 large heads of garlic, cut in half crosswise, plus 1 tablespoon finely chopped fresh garlic
> 1 tablespoon olive oil
> 1 teaspoon salt
> ¼ teaspoon freshly ground black pepper
> 1 large white onion, finely chopped
> 6 cups unsalted or reduced-sodium chicken broth
> Chopped fresh parsley, for garnish

1. Preheat the oven to 375° F. Place the halves of the garlic heads in a small baking pan, cut sides up, and drizzle ¼ teaspoon oil over each half. Season lightly with a little of the salt and pepper. Cover the pan tightly with aluminum foil and bake 50 to 60 minutes, until golden. Remove the foil and let stand until cool enough to handle. Squeeze the garlic from the skins (it will pop right out) and reserve.

2. Heat the remaining 2 teaspoons oil in a large nonstick skillet. Add the onion and cook over medium-high heat, stirring often, until golden, about 7 minutes. Add the chopped fresh garlic and cook until the garlic is just beginning to color, 2 to 3 minutes longer. Scrape the mixture into a blender or food processor. Add the reserved roasted garlic and 2 cups of the chicken broth. Purée until smooth.

3. Pour the roasted garlic and onion purée into a large saucepan. Whisk in the remaining 4 cups chicken broth and season with the remaining salt and pepper. Bring to a boil, reduce the heat and simmer, stirring occasionally, 15 minutes. Serve hot, garnished with chopped fresh parsley.

Mexican Vegetable Chowder

8 SERVINGS   130 CALORIES PER SERVING

1 large white onion, thinly sliced
1½ tablespoons olive oil
4 garlic cloves, thinly sliced
1 can (28 ounces) whole tomatoes in purée (see Note)
1 can (4 ounces) diced green chiles, drained
1 medium zucchini, cut into ½-inch dice
1 large chayote (also called vegetable pear or mirliton) or another
   zucchini, cut into ½-inch dice
2 celery ribs, thinly sliced
2 medium carrots, peeled and cut into ½-inch dice
1½ cups fresh, canned or frozen corn kernels
2 teaspoons dried marjoram or basil
1 bay leaf
6 cups unsalted or reduced-sodium chicken broth
½ teaspoon salt
½ teaspoon freshly ground black pepper

1. In a large saucepan or Dutch oven, cook the onion in the olive oil until the onion is soft, about 5 minutes. Add the garlic and cook until soft and fragrant, 1 to 2 minutes longer.

2. Add the tomatoes, chiles, zucchini, chayote, celery, carrots, corn, marjoram, bay leaf, chicken broth, salt and pepper. Bring to a boil, reduce the heat and simmer about 10 minutes, or until the vegetables are just tender.

NOTE *If you see them in your market, three 10-ounce cans of diced tomatoes and green chiles can be substituted for the 28-ounce can of tomatoes and the 4-ounce can of green chiles.*

Black Bean Soup

8 SERVINGS   200 CALORIES PER SERVING

¾ *pound dried black beans, rinsed and picked over to remove any grit*
1 *tablespoon olive oil*
1 *medium white onion, chopped*
6 *garlic cloves, chopped*
½ *to 1 teaspoon crushed hot red pepper, to taste*
3 *sprigs of fresh marjoram or 1½ teaspoons dried*
2 *teaspoons ground cumin*
1 *teaspoon ground coriander*
9 *cups unsalted or reduced-sodium chicken broth*
2 *tablespoons dry sherry (optional)*
2 *tablespoons sherry vinegar*
1½ *teaspoons salt*
½ *teaspoon freshly ground black pepper*
Diced white onion and chopped cilantro or fresh parsley, for garnish

1. In a large bowl, soak the black beans overnight in enough water to cover them by 3 inches. Alternatively, place the beans with the water in a large pot. Bring to a boil, cover and remove from the heat; let stand 1 hour. Drain the beans and rinse them well.

2. Heat the oil in a large saucepan or Dutch oven. Add the onion and cook over medium heat until softened, about 5 minutes. Add the garlic and crushed hot pepper and cook, stirring occasionally, until the garlic is softened and fragrant, about 2 minutes. Add the marjoram, cumin and coriander and cook, stirring, 1 minute.

3. Add the black beans and 8 cups of the chicken broth. Bring to a boil, reduce the heat and simmer until the beans have softened slightly, about 45 minutes. Add the remaining 1 cup broth, the sherry, sherry vinegar, salt and pepper. Continue simmering until the beans are soft, about 20 to 30 minutes. Let the soup stand 1 hour or refrigerate overnight to allow the flavors to blend.

4. Before serving, ladle 2 cups of the soup and ½ cup water into a food processor or blender and purée until smooth. Return to the soup and cook over medium heat, stirring often, until hot, about 5 minutes. Serve garnished with a sprinkling of the diced white onion and chopped cilantro.

Hearty Pinto Bean Soup

8 SERVINGS   167 CALORIES PER SERVING

1 large white onion, chopped
1 tablespoon olive oil
2 heads of garlic, cut in half
6 dried ancho chiles or ½ cup ground ancho chile powder
2 teaspoons chopped fresh marjoram or 1 teaspoon dried
1½ teaspoons fresh thyme leaves or ½ teaspoon dried
1 bay leaf
Pinch of ground clove
Pinch of ground coriander
Pinch of freshly grated nutmeg
8 cups unsalted or reduced-sodium chicken or beef broth
2 tablespoons cider vinegar
¾ teaspoon salt
½ teaspoon freshly ground black pepper
2 cans (16 ounces each) pinto beans, rinsed and drained
Finely chopped white onion, for garnish

1. In a large saucepan, cook the chopped onion in the olive oil over medium heat until the onion is soft, about 5 minutes. Add the garlic and cook until softened and fragrant, 1 to 2 minutes. Add the ancho chiles, marjoram, thyme, bay leaf, cloves, coriander, nutmeg, chicken broth, vinegar, salt and pepper. Bring to a boil, reduce the heat and simmer 15 minutes.

2. Add the pinto beans and cook 5 minutes longer. Let the soup stand for 1 hour at room temperature or refrigerate overnight to allow the flavors to blend.

3. Before serving, remove and discard the bay leaf. Fish out the whole chiles, if you used them. Remove the stems and seeds and purée the chiles with about ½ cup of the soup in a blender or food processor. Return the purée to the saucepan. Reheat the soup and thin it with a little water if necessary. Garnish with a sprinkling of the finely chopped onion.

Creamy Corn Soup

6 SERVINGS   119 CALORIES PER SERVING

> 3 cups fresh corn kernels (cut from about 6 ears) or 2 packages (10
>   ounces each) frozen kernel corn, thawed
> 2 teaspoons butter
> ½ cup chopped white onion
> 1 can (4 ounces) diced green chiles, drained
> 3 cups unsalted or reduced-sodium chicken broth
> 1½ teaspoons cornstarch
> 1 cup skim milk
> ½ teaspoon salt
> Pinch of freshly ground black pepper
> 2 tablespoons chopped fresh parsley, for garnish

1. Reserve ½ cup of the corn and set aside. In a medium nonstick skillet, melt the butter over medium heat. Add the onion and, if using fresh corn, the remaining corn. Raise the heat to medium-high and cook, stirring occasionally, until the onion is softened and the corn is lightly cooked, about 5 minutes. Transfer the onion and corn to a food processor. If you're using thawed frozen corn, add it at this point. Add the green chiles and purée until smooth.

2. In a large saucepan, combine the corn purée and the chicken broth. Bring to a boil, reduce the heat to medium-low and simmer 5 minutes.

3. Stir the cornstarch into ¼ cup of the skim milk until smooth. Stir into the soup. Add the reserved ½ cup corn and the remaining skim milk, salt and black pepper. Bring to a boil over medium-high heat, stirring until thickened. Reduce the heat to medium-low and simmer 5 minutes. Serve hot with a sprinkling of chopped fresh parsley over each bowl.

Chilled Cantaloupe Soup with Mint and Jalapeño Peppers

Cantaloupe is extremely nutritious—high in vitamins A and C and in potassium—and conspicuously low in calories. In this recipe, it is used to make an exceptionally refreshing soup that's something of a conversation piece and a cool way to start a summer meal.

6 SERVINGS   72 CALORIES PER SERVING

> 2 large ripe cantaloupes (about 5 pounds total)
> 3 fresh jalapeño or other hot green chile peppers
> 2 tablespoons fresh lime juice
> 2 tablespoons juice from a jar of pickled jalapeño peppers
> 1 teaspoon salt
> 2 tablespoons chopped fresh mint or 1 teaspoon dried

1. Peel and seed the melons. Cut them into 1- to 2-inch chunks. Cut the stems from the jalapeños and remove the seeds and ribs. Slice the jalapeños into thin strips.

2. In a blender or food processor, purée half the melon cubes, the jalapeños, lime juice, pickled jalapeño juice and salt. Pour the purée into a large bowl. Purée the remaining melon chunks and stir into the soup along with the mint. Cover and refrigerate for about 1 hour. Serve slightly chilled.

Chapter Three

TORTILLAS
IN
ALL
THEIR GLORY

If you're like many of my friends, this will be your favorite chapter in the book. There's something about that particular Mexican combination of corn, rice, beans and tortillas, tinged with the tart piquancy of lime juice and assorted salsas, that's just irresistibly appealing. And the healthful carbohydrates of this kind of food provide very much the same sort of comfort that pasta does in Italian cooking. In fact, the resemblance doesn't stop there.

It's often pointed out that pasta doesn't have to be fattening, and in the same way, tortilla dishes do not have to be heavy. Reducing fat in the ingredients and managing portion control is the key. Just as Americans make a main course out of heaping mounds of pasta while Italians eat a small portion as a first course, so Mexicans usually eat tacos, burritos and the like for a snack or light supper—since they eat their big meal at noon—while we pile them up on a plate with enough Spanish rice and refried beans to roll us out of any self-respecting restaurant.

In point of fact, a six- to seven-inch corn or flour tortilla contains only about 70 calories, roughly the same as a slice of bread. By using reduced-fat cheeses, modest but nutritiously sound amounts of protein and plenty of healthful, high-fiber vegetables to extend quantities, we can enjoy even this more traditional Mexican food anytime we want.

Accordingly, this chapter is full of tostadas, tacos, burritos and enchiladas of every sort, from Vegetarian Tostadas with Avocado and Cheese and Spicy Turkey Tacos to Potato and Cheese Flautas and Chicken Fajitas. I've even included a recipe for the classic Pico de Gallo salsa that goes with fajitas. The casseroles are particularly convenient for busy cooks because they can be assembled ahead and baked shortly before serving. And there are a number of tortilla recipes, such as Eggs Ranchero Style and Soft Tacos with Scrambled Eggs and Green Chiles, that are just right for a special breakfast or brunch.

All these recipes were developed for 400 calories or less. Many come in at under 300, and a few even skirt under 200, allowing plenty of room for a helping of Spanish Rice (p. 157) and my reduced-fat Refried Pinto Beans (p. 137).

— *Vegetarian Tostadas with Avocado and Cheese* —

Imagine tostadas as a kind of Mexican pizza. The tortillas are baked until crisp and topped with a delectable mound of tempting, low-calorie ingredients and palate pleasers. Most are appropriate for a light lunch. This all-vegetable version would also make a nice first course at a Mexican dinner, in place of an ordinary salad.

4 SERVINGS   202 CALORIES PER SERVING

> 4 flour tortillas (6 to 7 inches in diameter)
> 1½ tablespoons olive oil
> 1½ teaspoons red wine vinegar
> ¼ teaspoon salt
> ⅛ teaspoon freshly ground black pepper
> 1 cup finely shredded lettuce
> ¼ cup diced ripe tomato
> 2 teaspoons minced seeded fresh jalapeño or other green chile pepper
> ¼ cup canned vegetarian-style refried beans
> 6 tablespoons mashed ripe avocado
> ¼ cup crumbled reduced-fat goat cheese or feta or shredded reduced-fat
>   Monterey Jack or Cheddar
> 6 pitted jumbo olives, thinly sliced
> 4 thin slices of sweet onion, separated into rings

1. Preheat the oven to 375° F. Brush the tortillas lightly on both sides with 1½ teaspoons of the oil. Place on a baking sheet and bake until crisp and golden, 6 to 8 minutes.

2. In a small bowl, combine the remaining 1 tablespoon oil with the vinegar, salt, black pepper and 1 tablespoon plus 1 teaspoon water. Whisk or beat with a fork until well blended. In a medium bowl, toss the lettuce, tomato and jalapeño pepper. Pour the vinaigrette over the salad and toss.

3. Spread 1 tablespoon of the refried beans over each tortilla. Spread 2 tablespoons of the mashed avocado over the beans on each tostada. Top with the salad and garnish with the cheese, olive slices and onion rings.

Chicken Tostadas

Tostadas are crisply fried corn tortillas piled with layers of different fillings and eaten like open-faced sandwiches. There are as many variations as there are tastes, and with the "frying" changed to a very low-fat oven crisping, any number of them can be made for under 200 calories.

4 SERVINGS   201 CALORIES PER SERVING

> *½ pound skinless, boneless chicken breasts or skinless boneless turkey*
> *breast*
> *4 corn tortillas*
> *Vegetable cooking spray*
> *½ cup canned pinto beans, rinsed and drained*
> *Pinch of salt and freshly ground black pepper*
> *½ cup chopped white onion*
> *2 to 4 teaspoons seeded and minced fresh jalapeño or other hot green*
> *chile peppers, to taste*
> *1 cup shredded iceberg lettuce*
> *½ cup diced avocado (½ medium)*
> *1 medium tomato, diced*

1. Cut the chicken into 2-inch pieces. Place in a medium saucepan of lightly salted water and bring to a simmer over medium heat. Reduce the heat to medium-low and cook 10 to 15 minutes, or until the chicken is white throughout with no trace of pink in the center. Remove the pan from the heat and let the chicken cool in the liquid for at least 15 minutes. Then remove the chicken pieces and tear or cut into large shreds.

2. Meanwhile, preheat the oven to 375° F. Spray the corn tortillas lightly on both sides with vegetable cooking spray and place on a baking sheet. Bake until golden and crisp, 10 to 12 minutes.

3. Mash the pinto beans with a fork until they are coarsely puréed. Season the beans with the salt and pepper. Spread about 1½ tablespoons puréed beans over each warm tortilla. Scatter the chicken over the beans, dividing evenly. Top each with 2 tablespoons chopped onion, 1 teaspoon minced jalapeño pepper, ¼ cup shredded lettuce and 2 tablespoons each diced avocado and tomato. Serve at once so the tostada doesn't lose its crispness.

Variation

Chicken Tostada Melts: Make the Chicken Tostadas through step 2, but leave the oven on. Spread 1 tablespoon refried beans over each tortilla. Top with the shredded chicken. Then sprinkle 1 tablespoon shredded reduced-fat Cheddar cheese over the top of each, set the tortillas on a baking sheet and bake until the cheese melts, 3 to 5 minutes. Garnish each tostada with a thin slice of red onion, separated into rings, and serve hot, with ⅓ cup shredded lettuce and 2 tomato wedges on each plate.

4 Servings   181 Calories per serving

Jalapeño Pepper Tomato Sauce

Makes about 2 cups   34 Calories per ½ cup

> ¾ *pound plum tomatoes*
> 1 *medium white onion, thickly sliced*
> 3 *garlic cloves, peeled*
> 4 *fresh jalapeño or other hot green chile peppers, stems removed*
> ⅓ *cup unsalted or reduced-sodium chicken broth*
> 3 *tablespoons chopped cilantro or parsley*
> *Salt and freshly ground black pepper*

1. Preheat the broiler. Cover a baking sheet with aluminum foil and arrange the tomatoes, onion and garlic on it. Broil about 3 inches from the heat, turning the ingredients once, and removing them as they become lightly charred, about 8 to 10 minutes for the tomatoes, about 15 minutes for the onion and 6 to 8 minutes for the garlic. Let stand until cool.

2. If you don't want your sauce overly spicy, cut the jalapeño peppers in half and remove the seeds. Peel the skins from the tomatoes. Place the roasted tomatoes, onion and garlic in a food processor or blender. Add the chicken broth and purée until smooth.

3. Pour the purée into a medium nonaluminum saucepan, bring to a simmer over medium heat and cook, stirring occasionally, until reduced to a thick sauce, 10 to 12 minutes. Season with cilantro, salt and black pepper to taste.

Chili Beef Tostadas with Pickled Jalapeño Peppers

Yes, you can still enjoy beef on a diet, as long as it is the leanest you can buy and the portions are strictly controlled. Ground sirloin is the leanest; in most markets it is labeled 90 percent lean, but some trim up to 93 percent and a few as high as 95 percent lean. Since only a small amount is needed, the extra cost will be minimal.

4 SERVINGS   269 CALORIES PER SERVING

> 1 tablespoon corn or olive oil
> 1 small onion, chopped
> ½ pound ground sirloin (90% lean)
> 1½ teaspoons chili powder
> ½ teaspoon ground cumin
> ¼ teaspoon dried oregano
> ¼ teaspoon salt
> ⅛ teaspoon freshly ground black pepper
> ¼ cup refried beans
> 4 flour tortillas (6 to 7 inches in diameter)
> ¼ cup shredded reduced-fat Monterey Jack cheese
> 4 large pickled jalapeño peppers, thinly sliced
> 1 cup shredded fresh spinach
> ¼ cup low-fat sour cream
> 4 thin slices of red onion, separated into rings

1. Heat 1½ teaspoons of the oil in a large nonstick skillet over medium heat. Add the onion and cook, stirring occasionally, until the onion is soft and translucent, about 3 minutes. Add the ground beef and cook, stirring to break up any lumps of meat, until lightly browned. Add the chili powder, cumin, oregano, salt and pepper. Cook, stirring, 1 minute.

2. Add ¼ cup of water and cook, stirring occasionally, until the liquid is evaporated to a thick sauce, about 5 minutes. Stir the refried beans into the chili-flavored ground beef. Set aside.

3. Preheat the oven to 375° F. Brush the tortillas lightly with the remaining 1½ teaspoons oil. Place on a baking sheet and bake until crisp and golden, 6 to 8 minutes. Remove from the oven, but leave the oven on.

4. If the beef and bean filling has cooled, warm over medium-low heat until hot. Spread the filling over the tortillas, dividing evenly. Sprinkle 1 tablespoon of the cheese over each. Return the tostadas to the oven and bake 3 to 4 minutes, or until the cheese is melted. Sprinkle the sliced pickled jalapeño peppers and shredded spinach on the tostadas. Top with the sour cream and red onion rings and serve at once.

Shrimp Salad Tostadas

Lime-doused shrimp, creamy avocado and crunchy sweet red pepper make this a delightful starter or lunch dish.

4 SERVINGS   224 CALORIES PER SERVING

> ¼ cup fresh lime juice
> 2 tablespoons juice from pickled jalapeño peppers
> 1 tablespoon olive oil
> ⅛ teaspoon salt
> 6 ounces tiny frozen cooked shrimp, thawed and patted dry
> 1 small avocado, finely diced
> ⅓ cup finely diced red bell pepper
> 1 tablespoon minced seeded fresh jalapeño pepper (optional)
> 2 tablespoons finely diced red onion
> 1 medium tomato, finely diced
> 1 tablespoon chopped cilantro or parsley
> 4 corn tortillas
> Vegetable cooking spray
> 2 cups finely shredded lettuce

1. In a small bowl, combine the lime juice, jalapeño juice, olive oil and salt. Add the shrimp, avocado, red pepper, jalapeño, red onion, tomato and cilantro. Toss and set aside at room temperature for up to 30 minutes or cover and refrigerate, tossing occasionally, for up to 2 hours.

2. Preheat the oven to 375° F. Spray the tortillas lightly on both sides with vegetable cooking spray and place on a baking sheet. Bake until golden and crisp, 10 to 12 minutes.

3. To assemble the tostadas, top each toasted tortilla with ½ cup shredded lettuce. Mound the shrimp salad on top.

Garden Salad Tostadas

When you're counting calories, it's nice to have a special, especially low-calorie treat you can whip up at any time for a snack or simple lunch. These colorful tostadas look sumptuous, because they are heaped with an assortment of vegetables that spill out onto the plate, but the combination is light and exceptionally lean. There's not even any oil in the dressing.

4 SERVINGS   219 CALORIES PER SERVING

> 3 tablespoons cider vinegar
> 2 tablespoons fresh lime or lemon juice
> 2 tablespoons water
> 1 small garlic clove, crushed through a press
> 1 tablespoon sugar
> ¼ teaspoon salt
> ⅛ teaspoon freshly ground black pepper
> 4 corn tortillas
> Vegetable cooking spray
> 2 medium carrots, peeled
> 6 radishes
> 1 small cucumber
> 1 large tomato, finely diced
> 1 small avocado
> 1 cup shredded fresh spinach or lettuce
> ¼ cup crumbled reduced-fat feta cheese or shredded reduced-fat sharp
>   Cheddar
> ½ cup low-fat plain yogurt
> 4 pitted black olives, thinly sliced

1. In a medium bowl, mix together the vinegar, 1 tablespoon plus 2 teaspoons lime juice, the water, garlic, sugar, salt and black pepper. Stir the dressing until the sugar dissolves.

2. Preheat the oven to 375° F. Spray the corn tortillas lightly on both sides with vegetable cooking spray and place on a baking sheet. Bake until golden and crisp, 10 to 12 minutes.

3. Meanwhile, in a food processor fitted with the shredding disk or on the large holes of a hand grater, shred the carrots, radishes and cucumber. Add to the bowl with the dressing. Add the diced tomato and toss well to coat. Set aside for no more than 1 hour.

4. In a small bowl, mash the avocado coarsely. Blend in the remaining 1 teaspoon lime juice and season with a little additional salt and black pepper to taste.

5. To assemble the tostadas, spread one-fourth of the mashed avocado over each tortilla. Top each with ¼ cup of the shredded spinach and mound the tossed vegetables over the spinach, dividing evenly. Sprinkle 1 tablespoon cheese over each tostada, top with a dollop of yogurt and garnish with the olive slices.

Pickled Shrimp

4 SERVINGS   122 CALORIES PER SERVING

> 3 celery ribs, coarsely chopped
> 1 medium onion, unpeeled, cut into quarters
> 1 head of garlic, cut in half crosswise
> 12 whole allspice berries
> 12 black peppercorns
> 6 whole cloves
> 3 bay leaves
> ¼ cup Worcestershire sauce
> 8 sprigs of parsley
> 2 teaspoons crushed hot red pepper
> 1 pound large shrimp (about 24), shelled and deveined

1. In a large saucepan or Dutch oven, combine the celery, onion, garlic, allspice berries, peppercorns, cloves, bay leaves, Worcestershire sauce, parsley, hot pepper and 3 quarts of water. Bring to a boil over medium-high heat, reduce the heat and simmer 30 minutes. Strain and reserve the liquid.

2. Reheat the liquid to simmering. Add the shrimp and cook until they are pink, loosely curled and opaque throughout, about 3 minutes. Drain well. Serve at room temperature.

Soft Tacos with Pickled Shrimp

4 SERVINGS   254 CALORIES PER SERVING

Pickled Shrimp (p. 55)
½ medium white onion, thinly sliced (about ½ cup)
4 pickled jalapeño peppers, seeded and thinly sliced
1 tablespoon olive or corn oil
1 tablespoon white wine vinegar
1 tablespoon sugar
2 teaspoons prepared mustard
½ teaspoon hot pepper sauce
¼ teaspoon salt
¼ teaspoon freshly ground black pepper
4 corn tortillas
1 cup shredded iceberg lettuce or green cabbage
4 slices of red onion, separated into rings

1. Prepare the Pickled Shrimp and, while still warm, toss with the sliced white onion, pickled jalapeño peppers, oil, vinegar, sugar, mustard, hot sauce, salt and pepper. Let stand at room temperature about 30 minutes or cover and marinate for up to 2 hours. (If refrigerated, let return to room temperature before serving.)

2. Preheat the oven to 250° F. Shortly before serving time, wrap the corn tortillas in aluminum foil and bake until warmed through and soft, about 5 to 10 minutes.

3. Divide the shrimp among the warm tortillas and top with the lettuce or cabbage and the red onion rings. Fold the tortillas over the filling and serve.

Quesadillas with Roasted Peppers, Onions and Garlic

Packed with flavor, these quesadillas are amazingly light because of the goat cheese used in place of the traditional jack cheese. For an added fillip, pass a bowl of Jalapeño Pepper Tomato Sauce (p. 51) on the side.

4 SERVINGS   344 CALORIES PER SERVING

> *1 can (4 ounces) whole roasted green chiles, drained*
> *1 jar (4 ounces) roasted red peppers, drained*
> *Vegetable cooking spray*
> *1 medium white onion, thinly sliced*
> *1 large garlic clove, thinly sliced*
> *Pinch of salt and freshly ground black pepper*
> *4 ounces reduced-fat goat cheese or feta cheese, crumbled (about 1 cup)*
> *8 corn or flour tortillas (6 to 7 inches in diameter)*

1. Seed the green chiles. Cut the chiles and roasted red peppers into thin strips and set aside.

2. Spray a large nonstick skillet with vegetable cooking spray, add the onion and cook over medium heat until soft, about 5 minutes. Add the garlic and cook until the onion and garlic are lightly browned, 3 to 5 minutes. Add the red pepper and green chile strips to the onion and toss to mix. Season lightly with salt and black pepper to taste.

3. Preheat the oven to 325° F. Spray two baking sheets with vegetable cooking spray and arrange the tortillas on the sheets in a single layer. Sprinkle 2 tablespoons of the crumbled cheese over each tortilla. Spread the pepper, onion and garlic mixture over the goat cheese, dividing evenly.

4. Bake the quesadillas 8 to 10 minutes, or until the goat cheese has softened. Remove the quesadillas from the oven, fold each one in half and turn over. Bake 5 minutes longer, or until crisp and lightly browned. Allow 2 quesadillas per person.

Mushroom Quesadillas with Chipotle Tomato Sauce

If you have the opportunity to use "wild" mushrooms in this recipe—cremini, oyster or morels, for example—the flavor will be superb. However, these quesadilas are also wonderful just made with ordinary white button mushrooms.

4 SERVINGS   363 CALORIES PER SERVING

1 tablespoon olive oil
1 medium white onion, thinly sliced
1 garlic clove, minced
1 pound fresh mushrooms, sliced
1 tablespoon chopped cilantro or parsley
1 tablespoon chopped fresh oregano or 1 teaspoon dried
½ teaspoon salt
½ teaspoon freshly ground black pepper
4 ounces reduced-fat goat cheese or feta cheese, crumbled (about 1 cup)
8 corn tortillas
Vegetable cooking spray
Chipotle Tomato Sauce (recipe follows), as accompaniment
6 tablespoons plain low-fat yogurt or sour cream

1. Heat the olive oil in a large nonstick skillet over medium-high heat. Add the onion and cook until softened, 3 to 5 minutes. Add the garlic and mushrooms and cook, stirring often, until the mushrooms are lightly browned and any liquid they give off is evaporated, 5 to 7 minutes. Remove from the heat and stir in the cilantro, oregano, salt and ¼ teaspoon pepper. Set the mushrooms aside to cool slightly.

2. In a small bowl, mash the goat cheese with a fork. Blend in the remaining ¼ teaspoon black pepper.

3. Preheat the oven to 375° F. Wrap the corn tortillas in aluminum foil and bake until softened and hot, 10 to 15 minutes. Remove the tortillas from the oven and keep covered with a kitchen towel until you use them.

4. One at a time, place 2 tablespoons of the mushroom filling in the center of a warm corn tortilla. Dot with about 1 tablespoon of the seasoned goat cheese and fold the tortilla in half to form a half-moon shape. Secure the edges of the quesadilla with toothpicks in three spots. Repeat with the remaining filling, cheese and tortillas.

5. Spray a nonstick baking sheet with cooking spray and arrange the quesadillas on the sheet in a single layer. Lightly coat the quesadillas with the spray and bake 10 to 15 minutes, or until the quesadillas are crisp and lightly browned.

6. Allow 2 quesadillas per person. Top with ¼ cup of Chipotle Tomato Sauce if you like and a dollop of yogurt. Pass the remaining sauce on the side.

Chipotle Tomato Sauce

Chipotle peppers are smoked dried jalapeños. They are fiery hot and delightfully full of flavor. Just a small amount adds an entirely new dimension to a dish. This sauce goes especially well with the Mushroom Quesadillas, above; it is also very good as an alternative red sauce with Chicken Enchilada Casserole, p. 80. The recipe doubles easily.

MAKES ABOUT 2½ CUPS   30 CALORIES PER ¼ CUP

1 can (14 ounces) Italian-style plum tomatoes, with their juices
1 jar (4 ounces) roasted red peppers, drained
1 canned chipotle pepper in adobo sauce plus ½ teaspoon of the sauce
1 tablespoon olive oil
1 medium onion, chopped
3 garlic cloves, minced
1 bay leaf
2 teaspoons chopped fresh marjoram or ¾ teaspoon dried
2 teaspoons fresh thyme leaves or ½ teaspoon dried
½ teaspoon salt
¼ teaspoon freshly ground black pepper

1. In a food processor or blender, combine the tomatoes with their juices, the roasted red peppers and the chipotle pepper with its sauce. Purée until smooth.

2. In a large nonstick skillet, heat the oil over medium heat. Add the onion and garlic and cook until soft, about 3 minutes. Add the tomato-pepper purée, bay leaf, marjoram, thyme, salt and black pepper. Bring to a boil, reduce the heat to medium-low and simmer until thickened, 10 to 12 minutes. Remove and discard the bay leaf. Serve the sauce warm or at room temperature.

– "Roll Your Own" Chicken and Vegetable Tacos –

Vegetables are one important key to satisfying your hunger while restricting your intake of calories. A medium potato has only about 80 calories. Here potato and carrots are used to stretch chicken and add important vitamins and minerals.

6 Servings   382 Calories per serving

> 4 chicken breast halves on the bone (about 2 pounds)
> 2 tablespoons olive oil
> 3 garlic cloves, crushed through a press
> ½ teaspoon dried thyme
> ½ teaspoon dried marjoram or oregano
> 1 teaspoon salt
> ½ teaspoon freshly ground black pepper
> 4 carrots, peeled and cut into ½-inch slices
> 2 large baking potatoes (about 1 pound), peeled and cut into ½-inch dice
> 1 tablespoon white wine vinegar
> 12 flour tortillas (6 to 7 inches in diameter)
> Mexican Tomato Sauce (recipe follows) or mix 1 can (15 ounces) tomato sauce "special" (with tomato bits, onions, celery and green peppers added) with 1 jar (4 ounces) roasted red peppers, drained and puréed
> ¼ cup grated Parmesan cheese

1. Preheat the oven to 350° F. Remove the skin from the chicken and trim off any visible fat. Rinse and pat dry with paper towels. Line a baking sheet with aluminum foil and arrange the chicken on it in a single layer. In a small bowl, combine 1 tablespoon of the olive oil, the garlic, thyme, marjoram, ½ teaspoon salt and ¼ teaspoon black pepper. Rub the seasonings over the chicken breasts. Bake 30 to 35 minutes, or until no trace of pink remains at the center of the breasts. Remove from the oven and let cool.

2. While the chicken is baking, cook the carrots and potatoes separately in two medium saucepans of boiling salted water until tender but still firm, about 10 minutes for the potatoes, 5 to 7 for the carrots. Drain the vegetables well and combine them in a medium bowl. Sprinkle the remaining 1 tablespoon olive oil, the white wine vinegar, ½ teaspoon salt and ¼ teaspoon black pepper over the potatoes and carrots. Toss to coat well.

3. Wrap the tortillas in foil and warm them in the oven 10 to 15 minutes. Meanwhile, remove the chicken from the bones and cut into 2-inch strips. In a small nonaluminum saucepan, warm the sauce.

4. To serve, pour the sauce into a gravy boat. Place the vegetables, chicken and grated Parmesan cheese in separate dishes in the center of the table. Let your guests assemble their own tacos.

Mexican Tomato Sauce

This sauce keeps well in a covered container in the refrigerator for up to 5 days. If you cook Mexican food often, you may want to double the recipe and freeze half for another time.

MAKES 3½ TO 4 CUPS   20 CALORIES PER ¼ CUP

> *1 jar (4 ounces) roasted red peppers*
> *1 medium white onion, chopped*
> *1 tablespoon olive oil*
> *1 garlic clove, minced*
> *1 medium celery rib, chopped*
> *½ medium green bell pepper, chopped*
> *1 can (16 ounces) crushed tomatoes*
> *½ teaspoon salt*
> *¼ teaspoon freshly ground black pepper*

1. Drain the roasted red peppers and purée them in a blender or food processor. Set aside.

2. In a large nonstick skillet, cook the onion in the olive oil over medium heat until it begins to color, about 5 minutes. Add the garlic, celery and green pepper and cook until the vegetables have softened, about 5 minutes longer.

3. Add the tomatoes, salt and pepper. Simmer over medium heat, stirring often, until the sauce is thickened, 15 to 20 minutes.

Tacos Filled with Spicy Flaked Fish and Tomatillo Salsa

Tart and zesty, these unusual tacos make a satisfying light lunch on a hot summer day.

4 Servings   258 Calories per serving

> *1 pound firm-fleshed white fish fillets, such as snapper, tilefish or haddock*
> *2 cups unsalted or reduced-sodium chicken broth*
> *2 tablespoons juice from pickled jalapeño peppers*
> *1 tablespoon fresh lime juice*
> *¼ cup thinly sliced scallions*
> *1 medium tomato, finely diced*
> *¼ teaspoon salt*
> *⅛ teaspoon freshly ground black pepper*
> *8 store-bought taco shells*
> *1½ cups thinly shredded iceberg lettuce*
> *½ cup Tomatillo Salsa (p. 22) or bottled mild salsa verde, as accompaniment*

1. Halve or quarter the fish fillets, so they will fit in a medium saucepan. In the medium saucepan, combine the chicken broth, pickled jalapeño pepper juice and lime juice. Bring to a boil and reduce the heat to medium-low. Add the fish pieces and simmer 3 to 4 minutes. Remove the pan from the heat and let the fish cool in the liquid 30 minutes. Remove the fish and pat dry with paper towels.

2. Place the fish in a medium bowl and break the pieces into coarse flakes with your fingers or a fork. Add the scallions and tomato and toss the ingredients together. Season with the salt and pepper.

3. Arrange 2 tablespoons of the fish filling down the center of each taco shell. Divide the lettuce among the taco shells and top each taco with 1 tablespoon of the Tomatillo Salsa.

Spicy Beef Fajitas

The flavors of the marinade used for the beef and the smokiness added by grilling complement each other perfectly in this popular dish.

6 SERVINGS   290 CALORIES PER SERVING

> 2 canned chipotle peppers in adobo sauce, seeded and finely minced,
>   plus 1 tablespoon of the sauce
> 4 large garlic cloves, crushed through a press
> 3 tablespoons fresh lime juice
> 1 tablespoon olive oil
> ¾ teaspoon salt
> ½ teaspoon freshly ground black pepper
> 1½ pounds flank steak, well trimmed
> 6 flour tortillas (6 to 7 inches in diameter)
> 2 cups finely shredded iceberg lettuce
> 6 thin slices of red onion, separated into rings
> Fresh Tomato Salsa (p. 23), as accompaniment

1. In a small bowl, combine the chipotles and sauce, garlic, lime juice, oil, salt and black pepper. Mix well.

2. Place the flank steak in a large shallow glass dish. Brush the chipotle mixture over both sides of the steak. Cover with plastic wrap and let stand at room temperature for 1½ to 2 hours or refrigerate 12 hours or overnight.

3. Light a hot fire in a grill or preheat your broiler. When the fire is ready, wipe the marinade off the meat. Grill the steak or broil about 4 inches from the heat, turning once, 5 to 7 minutes per side, until rare or medium-rare, or longer to desired degree of doneness.

4. Transfer the steak to a carving board and let stand for 5 minutes before cutting crosswise on a slant into thin slices. Meanwhile, warm the flour tortillas on the grill for 1 to 2 minutes or wrap in aluminum foil and warm in the oven for 5 minutes. Serve the sliced flank steak with the warm tortillas and garnish with the lettuce, red onion rings and salsa.

Chicken Fajitas

Tortillas

64

Even when you're dieting, you can afford to embellish these light chicken fajitas with 1 tablespoon of Slim Guacamole (p. 20) and a half-serving each of Spanish Rice (p. 157) and Refried Pinto Beans (p. 137) and still come in at just over 400 calories.

6 SERVINGS   **217 CALORIES PER SERVING**

1½ pounds skinless, boneless chicken breasts
3 tablespoons fresh lime juice
1 tablespoon olive oil
1 garlic clove, crushed through a press
½ teaspoon dried oregano
¾ teaspoon salt
½ teaspoon freshly ground black pepper
6 flour tortillas (6 to 7 inches in diameter)
2 cups finely shredded lettuce
6 thin slices of red onion, separated into rings
Pico de Gallo (recipe follows), as accompaniment

1. Trim any visible fat from the chicken. Place in a glass dish and toss with the lime juice, oil, garlic, oregano, salt and pepper. Cover with plastic wrap and let stand at room temperature 30 minutes.

2. Meanwhile, preheat the oven to 350° F. and light a hot fire in a grill or preheat the broiler. Wrap the flour tortillas in aluminum foil and warm them in the oven 15 minutes.

3. Remove the chicken from the marinade and pat dry. Grill the chicken breasts or broil them 4 inches from the heat, turning once, until white throughout but still moist, 10 to 12 minutes.

4. Cut the chicken breasts crosswise on a slant into thin slices. Serve with the warmed tortillas and top with the lettuce and red onion rings. Pass the Pico de Gallo on the side.

Pico de Gallo

This is a spicy garnish usually served with fajitas. The name *pico de gallo* literally means "rooster's beak." The recipe is in between a salsa and a relish.

MAKES ABOUT 3 CUPS   47 CALORIES PER ¼ CUP

> 1 pound ripe tomatoes, finely diced
> ¼ to ⅓ cup minced seeded jalapeño peppers
> 1 large white onion, finely chopped
> 1 large avocado, finely diced
> ¼ cup chopped cilantro or parsley
> 2 tablespoons fresh lime juice
> 2 tablespoons juice from pickled jalapeño peppers
> 1 teaspoon salt

In a medium bowl, combine the tomatoes, jalapeño peppers, onion, avocado, cilantro, lime juice, jalapeño juice and salt. Let stand 30 minutes to mellow the flavors. Serve at room temperature or slightly chilled.

Lamb Fajitas with Cucumber Relish

Lamb is often eaten as a special dish at fiestas in Mexico. Since variety is important when you are watching what you eat, I created this tantalizing lamb version of fajitas, and lightened it with a refreshing cucumber yogurt relish that is dolloped right on top of them. Charcoal grilling give these an extraordinary flavor, but if that's not possible, broil the steaks instead.

6 SERVINGS   260 CALORIES PER SERVING

> *1½ pounds boneless lamb steaks cut from the leg, about ½ inch thick, trimmed of all fat*
> *1 tablespoon olive oil*
> *3 large garlic cloves, thinly sliced*
> *1 tablespoon minced fresh rosemary or 1 teaspoon dried*
> *½ teaspoon salt*
> *½ teaspoon freshly ground black pepper*
> *12 corn or flour tortillas (6 to 7 inches in diameter)*
> *2 cups finely shredded fresh spinach*
> *1 cup Cucumber Relish (recipe follows)*

1. Put the lamb steaks in a shallow dish large enough to hold them in a single layer. Brush them with the olive oil and sprinkle the garlic, rosemary, salt and pepper over the meat. Cover with plastic wrap and marinate at room temperature for 1 hour or up to 24 hours in the refrigerator. (If the lamb is chilled, remove it from the refrigerator about 30 minutes before cooking.)

2. Meanwhile, light a hot fire in a charcoal grill. It will take about 40 minutes for the coals to reach the right temperature. When you're about 10 minutes away from grilling the meat, preheat the oven to 350° F. Wrap the flour tortillas in aluminum foil and warm them in the oven 15 minutes.

3. Grill the lamb steaks, turning them once, about 3 to 5 minutes on each side, or until medium-rare to medium, or longer if you prefer. Cut the steaks crosswise into thin strips and divide among the tortillas. Garnish the meat with shredded spinach and Cucumber Relish.

Cucumber Relish

MAKES 3 CUPS   26 CALORIES PER ⅓ CUP

1 medium cucumber, peeled, seeded and finely diced
½ medium white onion, diced
1 medium tomato, diced
2 to 3 fresh jalapeño peppers, seeded and minced
1 tablespoon chopped cilantro or parsley
1 tablespoon chopped mint (optional)
2 teaspoons chopped fresh marjoram or oregano or 1 teaspoon dried
½ teaspoon salt
Juice of 1 lime
1 cup plain low-fat yogurt, whisked until smooth

In a medium bowl, combine the cucumber, onion, tomato, jalapeño peppers, cilantro, mint, marjoram, salt, lime juice and yogurt. Let stand 20 minutes. Stir and serve.

Beef Tacos

Yes, you can enjoy beef tacos even when you're counting calories. Here is a quick, easy version.

6 SERVINGS   384 CALORIES PER SERVING

12 store-bought taco shells
Beef Taco Filling (recipe follows), warmed
3 cups finely shredded lettuce
1 small onion, finely chopped
¾ cup (about 3 ounces) coarsely grated reduced-fat Cheddar or
*   Monterey Jack cheese*
¾ cup Homemade Salsa (p. 22), or your favorite bottled salsa

Preheat the oven to 350° F. Arrange the taco shells on a baking sheet. Toast the shells in the oven 5 to 7 minutes, until heated through. Fill each shell with ¼ cup beef filling and ¼ cup shredded lettuce. Sprinkle with chopped onion and 1 tablespoon cheese. Top each taco with 1 tablespoon salsa. Allow 2 tacos per person.

Beef Taco Filling

6 SERVINGS   155 CALORIES PER SERVING

Vegetable cooking spray
1 medium white onion, chopped
2 garlic cloves, minced
1 pound ground beef (90% lean)
1 can (14 ounces) crushed tomatoes
½ to 1 teaspoon crushed hot red pepper, to taste
1 teaspoon dried oregano
½ teaspoon ground cumin
¼ teaspoon ground cinnamon
⅛ teaspoon ground cloves
1 bay leaf
2 teaspoons cider vinegar
½ teaspoon salt

1. Spray a large nonstick skillet with vegetable cooking spray and cook the onion over medium heat, stirring often, until softened, 4 to 5 minutes. Add the garlic and cook 2 minutes longer.

2. Crumble the ground beef into the pan and cook, stirring to break up any lumps of meat, until the beef is no longer pink, 5 to 7 minutes. Stir in the tomatoes, hot pepper, oregano, cumin, cinnamon, cloves, bay leaf, cider vinegar and salt. Bring to a boil, reduce the heat to medium-low and simmer, stirring occasionally, until thickened, 20 to 25 minutes. Remove and discard the bay leaf before serving.

Baked Enchiladas with Red Chile Sauce

The enchilada got its name from the Mexican custom of dipping these filled tortillas into a sauce made from chiles.

6 SERVINGS   380 CALORIES PER SERVING

12 corn tortillas
1 medium onion, thinly sliced
1 tablespoon olive oil

1 garlic clove, minced
2 cups cooked white or brown rice
1 medium ripe tomato, diced
2 tablespoons chopped cilantro or parsley
½ teaspoon salt
¼ teaspoon freshly ground black pepper
Vegetable cooking spray
*Red Chile Sauce (recipe follows) or 2 cans (10 ounces each) enchilada
  sauce*
1½ cups shredded reduced-fat Cheddar (6 ounces)

1. Preheat the oven to 350° F. Divide the tortillas into 2 stacks and wrap each stack in aluminum foil. Place in the oven and bake until heated through and soft, about 10 minutes.

2. Meanwhile, in a large nonstick skillet, cook the onion in the oil over medium heat until softened, about 3 minutes. Add the garlic and cook until soft and fragrant, 1 to 2 minutes longer. Scrape the onion and garlic into a medium bowl. Add the rice, tomato, cilantro, salt and pepper. Mix well.

3. Spray a 9 × 13-inch baking dish or 12-inch oval gratin with vegetable cooking spray. Place 2 tablespoons of the rice filling in each of the warm tortillas, roll up and place them side by side, seam side down, in the baking dish. Pour the Red Chile Sauce over the enchiladas and sprinkle the cheese evenly over the top. Bake 20 to 25 minutes, or until the enchiladas are heated through and the cheese is melted and lightly browned. Serve hot.

Red Chile Sauce

MAKES ABOUT 2¼ CUPS   26 CALORIES PER ¼ CUP

2 garlic cloves, minced
1½ tablespoons olive oil
½ cup ground ancho chile powder or pure chile powder
3 cups unsalted or reduced-sodium chicken broth or water
½ to 1 teaspoon salt

1. In a large nonstick skillet, cook the garlic in the olive oil over medium heat, stirring often, until golden, 3 to 4 minutes; do not burn. Add the ground ancho chile powder and cook, stirring constantly, 1 minute.

2. Gradually whisk the chicken broth into the chile paste. Season with the salt and simmer, stirring often, until the sauce thickens, 8 to 10 minutes. If the sauce gets too thick, thin with a little broth or water.

Spicy Turkey Tacos

The early Spanish explorers brought turkeys back home from Mexico, where the Aztecs raised them for food. The birds got the name they did because the people in Europe thought the explorers had landed somewhere near Turkey, and not on an unknown continent. Like chicken, turkey is an exceptionally lean meat, very low in cholesterol.

4 SERVINGS   281 CALORIES PER SERVING

> *8 corn tortillas*
> *½ pound cooked skinless, boneless turkey breast, torn into shreds*
> *½ medium white onion, minced*
> *1 small tomato, finely diced*
> *1 tablespoon juice from pickled jalapeño peppers*
> *Salt and freshly ground black pepper*
> *1 cup shredded iceberg lettuce*
> *½ cup coarsely grated reduced-fat Monterey Jack cheese (about 2 ounces)*
> *½ cup bottled salsa*

1. Preheat the oven to 350° F. Wrap the tortillas in aluminum foil and warm them in the oven 10 to 15 minutes.

2. Meanwhile, in a medium bowl, toss together the turkey, onion, tomato and jalapeño juice. Season lightly with salt and pepper.

3. Put 2 tablespoons of the turkey mixture at the center of each warm tortilla. Top with 2 tablespoons shredded lettuce, 1 tablespoon grated cheese and 1 tablespoon bottled salsa. Fold the tortillas over the fillings in a taco shape. Allow 2 per person.

Corn Tortillas with Avocado and Tomato

1 SERVING   268 CALORIES PER SERVING

> *2 corn tortillas*
> *¼ cup finely shredded lettuce*
> *2 very thin slices of red onion*

1 small tomato, cut into 4 wedges
¼ avocado, cut into 4 thin slices
1 fresh jalapeño pepper, stemmed, seeded and cut lengthwise into thin
    slivers
1 tablespoon crumbled feta cheese
¼ of a fresh lime
Salt

1. Preheat the oven to 350° F. Wrap the tortillas in aluminum foil and warm in the oven for 10 minutes, or until softened.

2. To assemble, place half of the lettuce on each of the 2 tortillas. Top the lettuce with slices of red onion, tomato, avocado and slivers of jalapeño pepper. Sprinkle the feta cheese over the vegetables and squeeze fresh lime juice over the top. Season the tostadas with salt to taste and serve.

Soft Tacos with Scrambled Eggs and Green Chiles

4 SERVINGS   227 CALORIES PER SERVING

8 corn tortillas
4 eggs
¼ teaspoon salt
¼ teaspoon freshly ground black pepper
Vegetable cooking spray
1 can (4 ounces) diced green chiles, drained
½ medium red onion, finely chopped
½ cup bottled salsa

1. Preheat the oven to 350° F. Wrap the corn tortillas in aluminum foil and warm in the oven 15 minutes.

2. In the meantime, beat the eggs with 1 tablespoon water and the salt and pepper until just mixed.

3. Coat a large nonstick skillet with vegetable cooking spray. Add the green chiles and red onion and cook over medium heat, stirring often, until the onion is softened, 3 to 5 minutes. Add the beaten eggs and cook, stirring frequently, until set, about 3 minutes.

4. Place 2 to 3 tablespoons of the egg filling in the center of a warm tortilla and fold in half. Repeat for the other tortillas. Place 2 filled tortillas on 4 plates and top each serving with 2 tablespoons of salsa.

Brunch Tortillas with Eggs, Black Beans, Ham and Cheese

6 SERVINGS   274 CALORIES PER SERVING

6 corn tortillas
Vegetable cooking spray
1 small onion, minced
1 garlic clove, minced
1½ cups canned black beans, rinsed and drained
6 large eggs
Salt and freshly ground black pepper, to taste
2 cups Mexican Tomato Sauce (p. 61) or your favorite prepared brand
6 tablespoons chopped boiled ham
6 tablespoons shredded reduced-fat Cheddar or Monterey Jack cheese

1. Preheat the oven to 350° F. Wrap the corn tortillas in aluminum foil and warm in the oven 10 to 15 minutes. Meanwhile, coat a large nonstick skillet with vegetable cooking spray and cook the onion and garlic over medium heat until the onion is softened, 3 to 4 minutes. Add the black beans and cook, stirring and mashing with a fork or wooden spoon, until the beans are heated through and coarsely puréed, about 3 minutes. Remove from the heat and cover to keep warm.

2. Wipe out the skillet and coat again with the cooking spray. Fry the eggs in 3 batches, two at a time, over medium heat to desired degree of doneness. Season lightly with salt and pepper.

3. Place a warmed tortilla on each of 6 plates and spread ¼ cup of the warm beans over each tortilla. Top with an egg and coat lightly with ⅓ cup sauce. Sprinkle 1 tablespoon each ham and cheese over the top of each. Serve immediately.

Seafood Burritos with Green Sauce

4 SERVINGS   252 CALORIES PER SERVING

1 tablespoon plus 2 teaspoons olive oil
1 medium white onion, chopped, plus ¼ cup minced white onion
2 small garlic cloves, minced
2 cans (4 ounces each) diced green chiles, drained
⅓ cup unsalted or reduced-sodium chicken broth
½ teaspoon salt
4 flour tortillas (6 to 7 inches in diameter)
½ pound medium shrimp, shelled and deveined
½ pound medium sea scallops, cut in half
1 tablespoon chopped cilantro or parsley
1 cup shredded lettuce

1. Preheat the oven to 350° F. Heat the 2 teaspoons oil in a small saucepan. Add the ¼ cup minced onion and half the minced garlic and cook over medium heat, stirring, until just softened, 2 to 3 minutes. Add the chiles, chicken broth and ¼ teaspoon salt. Simmer, stirring often, 3 minutes. Purée the green sauce in a blender or food processor. Return to the saucepan, reheat over low heat if necessary and cover to keep warm.

2. Wrap the flour tortillas in aluminum foil and warm in the oven for 5 to 10 minutes.

3. Meanwhile, heat the remaining 1 tablespoon oil in a large nonstick skillet. Add the chopped onion and cook over medium-high heat until softened, about 3 minutes. Add the remaining garlic and cook 1 minute longer. Add the shrimp and scallops to the skillet and cook, tossing, until opaque in the center, 3 to 5 minutes.

4. Add the cilantro to the seafood and toss to mix. Season with the remaining ¼ teaspoon of salt. Fill each of the tortillas with one-fourth of the cooked shrimp and scallops and roll up the tortilla around the filling. Spread ¼ cup shredded lettuce on each serving plate, put a burrito on top of the lettuce and coat with ¼ to ⅓ cup green sauce.

— *Burritos with Ham and Rice Salad Stuffing* —

4 SERVINGS   256 CALORIES PER SERVING

8 corn tortillas
1 cup cooked white or brown rice
½ cup finely diced ham, preferably Black Forest (2 ounces)
¼ cup frozen peas, thawed
¼ cup finely diced carrot
¼ cup finely chopped celery
¼ cup diced tomato
2 tablespoons thinly sliced scallions
2 tablespoons chopped fresh parsley
½ teaspoon dried oregano
¼ teaspoon ground cumin
½ teaspoon salt
Pinch of cayenne pepper
1 cup shredded lettuce
½ cup bottled taco sauce or salsa

1. Preheat the oven to 350° F. Wrap the corn tortillas in 2 stacks in aluminum foil and warm in the oven for 10 to 15 minutes.

2. Meanwhile, in a large bowl, combine the rice, ham, peas, carrot, celery, tomato, scallions, parsley, oregano, cumin, salt and cayenne. Toss the mixture thoroughly.

3. Divide the rice salad evenly among the warm tortillas. Top each with ¼ cup shredded lettuce and 1 tablespoon taco sauce or salsa, and roll up.

Vegetarian Burritos with Black Beans and Avocado

4 SERVINGS   309 CALORIES PER SERVING

4 flour tortillas (6 to 7 inches in diameter)
1 cup cooked brown or white rice
½ cup canned black beans, rinsed and drained
¼ cup canned diced green chiles
¼ cup canned whole kernel corn
2 tablespoons thinly sliced scallions
2 tablespoons chopped cilantro or parsley
¼ teaspoon salt
¼ teaspoon freshly ground black pepper
1 medium avocado, diced
½ cup shredded reduced-fat Cheddar or Monterey Jack cheese (2 ounces)
1 cup shredded lettuce
½ cup bottled salsa

1. Preheat the oven to 350° F. Wrap the flour tortillas in aluminum foil and warm in the oven for 5 to 10 minutes until heated through.

2. Meanwhile, in a large bowl, combine the rice, beans, green chiles, corn, scallions, cilantro, salt and pepper. Toss to mix.

3. Divide the rice and bean salad evenly among the warm tortillas. Top each with one-fourth of the diced avocado, 2 tablespoons cheese, ¼ cup shredded lettuce and 1 tablespoon salsa. Roll up and eat.

Scrambled Egg Burritos with Potatoes and Chipotle Peppers

With their distinctive smoky flavor, chipotle peppers make this simple dish a masterpiece. If canned chipotles in adobo sauce are not available in your neighborhood, replace them with ½ teaspoon of crushed hot red pepper.

4 SERVINGS   325 CALORIES PER SERVING

½ pound red potatoes, cut into ½-inch dice
8 corn or flour tortillas (6 to 7 inches in diameter)
4 large eggs
½ teaspoon salt
½ medium white onion, chopped
1 tablespoon olive oil
1 garlic clove, minced
2 canned chipotle peppers, minced, plus 1 teaspoon of the adobo sauce
*   from the can, or ½ teaspoon crushed hot red pepper*
2 cups shredded lettuce
1 cup Fresh Tomato Salsa (p. 23), as accompaniment

1. Preheat the oven to 350° F. In a medium saucepan of boiling water, cook the potatoes until tender but not falling apart, 6 to 8 minutes. Drain the potatoes in a colander and rinse under cold running water to cool them. Leave the potatoes in the colander to drain.

2. Wrap the tortillas in aluminum foil and warm them in the oven 10 to 15 minutes.

3. Meanwhile, beat the eggs with the salt and 1 tablespoon water until just mixed. Set aside.

4. In a large nonstick skillet, cook the onion in the olive oil over medium-high heat until soft, 3 to 4 minutes. Add the garlic and cook until soft and fragrant, 1 to 2 minutes. Add the diced potatoes, reduce the heat to medium and cook, stirring frequently, until the potatoes are golden, 8 to 10 minutes. Add the minced chipotles and sauce and stir to mix well.

5. Add the beaten eggs to the skillet and lightly fold them together with the pepper mixture. Cook, stirring, until the eggs are just set, about 3 minutes. To serve, fill each of the warm tortillas with one-fourth of the cooked egg mixture, roll the tortilla around the filling and top with ¼ cup shredded lettuce and 1 tablespoon salsa.

— *Breakfast Burritos with Zucchini and Corn* —

4 SERVINGS   153 CALORIES PER SERVING

4 flour tortillas (6 to 7 inches in diameter)
2 whole large eggs
4 egg whites
Vegetable cooking spray
2 tablespoons finely chopped onion
1 small garlic clove, minced
1 small zucchini, cut into ¼-inch dice
1 can (4 ounces) whole kernel corn, drained
¼ teaspoon salt
Pinch of cayenne pepper
1 cup shredded lettuce
¼ cup of your favorite bottled salsa

1. Preheat the oven to 350° F. Wrap the flour tortillas in aluminum foil and warm them in the oven for 5 to 10 minutes until heated through.

2. Meanwhile, break the eggs into a medium bowl and add the whites. Mix the eggs with a fork just until blended.

3. Coat a medium nonstick skillet with vegetable cooking spray. Add the onion and cook over medium heat until the onion has softened, about 3 minutes. Add the garlic and zucchini and cook, stirring often, until the zucchini is crisp-tender, 2 to 3 minutes longer. Add the corn, egg mixture, salt and cayenne. Cook, stirring, until the eggs start to thicken, 3 to 4 minutes. Reduce the heat to low and cook to desired doneness.

4. To serve, fill each of the warm tortillas with one-fourth of the cooked egg mixture, roll the tortilla around the filling and top with ¼ cup shredded lettuce and 1 tablespoon salsa.

– Breakfast Burritos with Pinto Beans and Salsa –

4 SERVINGS   156 CALORIES PER SERVING

4 flour tortillas (6 to 7 inches in diameter)
2 whole large eggs
4 egg whites
¼ teaspoon dried oregano
¼ teaspoon ground cumin
¼ teaspoon salt
⅛ teaspoon freshly ground black pepper
Pinch of cayenne pepper
2 tablespoons thinly sliced scallions
½ cup canned pinto beans, rinsed and drained
Vegetable cooking spray
1 cup shredded lettuce
¼ cup of your favorite bottled salsa

1. Preheat the oven to 350° F. Wrap the flour tortillas in aluminum foil and warm them in the oven for 5 to 10 minutes until heated through.

2. Meanwhile, break the eggs into a medium bowl and add the whites. Mix the eggs with a fork just until blended. Mix in the oregano, cumin, salt, black pepper and cayenne. Add the scallions and pinto beans.

3. Coat a nonstick skillet with vegetable cooking spray. Add the egg mixture and cook over medium heat, stirring with a wooden spoon, until the eggs start to thicken, 3 to 4 minutes. Reduce the heat to low and cook to desired doneness.

4. To serve, fill each of the warm tortillas with one-fourth of the cooked egg mixture, roll the tortilla around the filling and top with ¼ cup shredded lettuce and 1 tablespoon salsa.

Eggs Ranchero Style

4 Servings   169 Calories per serving

1 cup Mexican Tomato Sauce (p. 61) or 1 can (8 ounces) tomato
*   sauce with green chiles*
4 corn tortillas
Vegetable cooking spray
4 large eggs
Salt and freshly ground black pepper
1 tablespoon plus 1 teaspoon crumbled feta or grated Parmesan cheese
1 tablespoon plus 1 teaspoon chopped cilantro or parsley

1. Warm the tomato sauce in a small nonaluminum saucepan over medium heat. Keep warm over low heat.

2. In a large nonstick skillet, cook the tortillas over medium-low heat, turning once, about 1 minute per side, until soft and warm. Wrap the tortillas in aluminum foil to keep them warm.

3. Wipe out the skillet and coat with vegetable cooking spray. Fry the eggs, 2 at a time, over medium heat to the desired degree of doneness. Season lightly with salt and pepper.

4. Place a warm tortilla on each of 4 serving plates. Top each with a fried egg. Spoon ¼ cup of the sauce over each egg and sprinkle 1 teaspoon cheese and 1 teaspoon chopped cilantro on top. Serve immediately.

Chicken Enchilada Casserole

Because of its mild nature, this dish makes a wonderful meal for children. If you'd like to spice it up a bit, substitute the Chipotle Tomato Sauce (p. 59) for the Mexican Tomato Sauce called for in this recipe.

8 SERVINGS   358 CALORIES PER SERVING

> *1 pound skinless, boneless chicken breasts*
> *1 large white onion, thinly sliced*
> *1 tablespoon olive oil*
> *1 cup reduced-fat ricotta cheese*
> *⅓ cup reduced-fat sour cream*
> *2 cans (7 ounces each) diced green chiles*
> *¼ teaspoon salt*
> *¼ teaspoon freshly ground black pepper*
> *12 corn tortillas*
> *Vegetable cooking spray*
> *Mexican Tomato Sauce (p. 61)*
> *1½ cups coarsely grated reduced-fat Monterey Jack cheese or Cheddar*
> *(6 ounces)*

1. Preheat the oven to 350° F. Trim any visible fat from the chicken. Place in a medium saucepan of lightly salted water and bring to a simmer over medium-high heat. Reduce the heat to medium-low and simmer until the chicken is white throughout with no trace of pink in the center but still moist, 10 to 15 minutes. Let the chicken stand in the liquid until cool enough to handle, then tear or cut into ½-inch-thick strips.

2. Meanwhile, in a large nonstick skillet, cook the onion in the olive oil over medium-high heat, stirring often, until beginning to color, about 5 minutes. Transfer to a medium bowl. Add the ricotta cheese, sour cream and green chiles and blend well. Add salt and pepper.

3. Spray the tortillas lightly on both sides with vegetable cooking spray. Arrange in a single layer on 2 baking sheets and bake until warm and softened, 6 to 8 minutes. Stack the warm tortillas on a plate. Leave the oven on.

4. Spray a 9 × 13-inch baking dish with the cooking spray and line the bottom with 4 tortillas, slightly overlapping. Spread half of the ricotta cheese mixture over the tortillas. Scatter half of the shredded chicken over the filling. Spoon on one-third of the tomato sauce. Sprinkle ½ cup of the cheese over the sauce. Make another layer of 4 tortillas, the remaining chicken, half

of the remaining tomato sauce and ½ cup of the cheese. Cover with the last 4 tortillas, ladle on the remaining sauce and sprinkle the remaining ½ cup cheese on top. Bake 30 minutes, or until the casserole is heated through.

Potato and Cheese Flautas

4 SERVINGS   275 CALORIES PER SERVING

½ pound red potatoes, peeled and cut into ½-inch dice
2 teaspoons corn or olive oil
½ medium white onion, chopped
1 garlic clove, minced
1 can (4 ounces) diced green chiles, drained
¼ teaspoon salt
⅛ teaspoon freshly ground black pepper
8 corn tortillas
¾ cup coarsely grated reduced-fat Cheddar (3 ounces)
Vegetable cooking spray
Shredded green cabbage and thinly sliced radishes, for garnish

1. In a medium saucepan of boiling salted water, cook the potatoes over medium-high until tender, 7 to 10 minutes. Drain and rinse briefly under cold running water; drain well.

2. Heat the oil in a large nonstick skillet. Add the onion and cook over medium heat until soft and just beginning to color, about 5 minutes. Add the garlic and cook, stirring often, 2 to 3 minutes. Add the potatoes and green chiles and cook, tossing, 2 minutes. Season with the salt and black pepper. Transfer the mixture to a small bowl and set aside.

3. Preheat the oven to 350° F. Wrap the corn tortillas in aluminum foil and heat in the oven 10 to 15 minutes, until softened.

4. Assemble the flautas one at a time. Place 2 tablespoons of the filling down the center of each tortilla. Sprinkle 1½ tablespoons of the grated cheese over the top of the filling. Roll the tortilla into a cigar shape and secure the edge with a toothpick. Continue this procedure until all the tortillas are filled.

5. Spray a baking sheet with vegetable cooking spray and arrange the flautas on the sheet in a single layer. Spray the flautas lightly with the cooking spray and bake for 6 to 8 minutes. Turn the flautas over and bake 6 to 8 minutes longer, until crisp and golden. Remove the toothpicks. Allow 2 flautas per person and garnish with shredded cabbage and sliced radishes.

Enchiladas Suizas Casserole

Skim milk and reduced-fat cheese make this Mexican favorite possible, even on a low-calorie diet. You may find you like this lighter version so much that you'll use it all the time.

6 Servings   389 Calories per serving

> *1 pound skinless, boneless chicken breasts*
> *2 cups Tomatillo Salsa (p. 22) or mild or medium bottled salsa verde*
> *½ cup reduced-fat sour cream*
> *1 cup skim milk*
> *1 cup (about 4 ounces) shredded reduced-fat Monterey Jack cheese*
> *½ cup shredded reduced-fat Cheddar*
> *12 corn tortillas*
> *1 cup corn kernels*

1. Trim any visible fat from the chicken. Place in a medium saucepan of lightly salted water and bring to a simmer over medium heat. Reduce the heat to medium-low and simmer 10 to 15 minutes, until the chicken is white throughout with no trace of pink in the center but still moist. Let cool in the liquid, then tear the chicken into large shreds.

2. Preheat the oven to 350° F. In a food processor or blender, combine the salsa, sour cream and milk. Process until blended.

3. Toss the two cheeses together. Coat the bottom of a medium gratin or 9 × 13-inch baking dish with a little of the sauce. Arrange 4 of the tortillas in the bottom of the dish, overlapping slightly or tearing as necessary to fit. Scatter half the chicken shreds, ½ cup corn and ½ cup cheese over the tortillas. Drizzle 1 cup sauce evenly over all. Cover with 4 more tortillas and layer on the remaining chicken and corn and another ½ cup cheese. Drizzle on another 1 cup sauce. Top with the remaining tortillas and pour on the remaining sauce. Sprinkle the remaining cheese on top. Bake until the filling is heated through and the cheese is golden brown, about 30 minutes.

Chilaquiles

In Mexico, this casserole is often made with leftover cooked chicken or turkey. It is an informal dish that might be served for lunch or a family supper.

6 Servings   267 Calories per serving

1 pound skinless, boneless chicken breasts
8 corn tortillas
Vegetable cooking spray
1 large white onion, thinly sliced
2 tablespoons chopped cilantro or parsley
½ recipe Mexican Tomato Sauce (p. 61) or 2 cups of your favorite
    prepared tomato sauce, preferably with green chiles added
1 cup coarsely grated reduced-fat mozzarella cheese

1. Place the chicken breasts in a medium saucepan of lightly salted water. Bring to a simmer over medium-high heat, reduce the heat to medium-low and simmer, 10 to 15 minutes, until the chicken is white throughout with no trace of pink in the center but still moist. Let the chicken stand in the broth until cool enough to handle, then tear or cut into shreds.

2. Preheat the oven to 375° F. Cut the tortillas in half and cut each half into 3 equal triangles. Place the tortilla triangles in a bowl, spray them lightly with vegetable cooking spray, toss and spread them on a baking sheet in a single layer. Bake 10 to 12 minutes, until pale golden and very crisp. Remove from the oven and let cool. Reduce the oven heat to 325° F.

3. While the tortillas are cooling, coat a large nonstick skillet with the cooking spray. Add the onion and cook over medium heat until softened and starting to turn golden at the edges, about 5 minutes. Toss the browned onion with the chicken shreds and chopped cilantro.

4. Coat a 9 × 13-inch baking dish with the cooking spray. Scatter the crisp tortilla triangles over the bottom of the dish. Pour the sauce over the tortilla chips and cover with the chicken, pressing it into the sauce. Sprinkle the cheese over the top. Bake the chilaquiles 20 to 25 minutes, or until the sauce is bubbling hot and the cheese is melted and lightly browned.

Chapter Four

SEAFOOD
MEXICAN STYLE

With nearly 3,000 miles of coastline, as well as numerous lakes and rivers, Mexico is a seafood lover's dream. Even in Mexico City, which lies in the center of the country about 200 miles from either coast, the markets are full of glistening fish and shellfish of all description—red snapper, striped bass, pompano, tuna, shrimp, clams, squid—flown and trucked in daily. This tradition goes back over 500 years, to the reigning days of the Aztecs, when their great king, Montezuma, who lived in the mountains just west of what is now Mexico City, arranged for teams of relay runners to speed fresh fish in from the oceans.

Such a national fondness for fish has, of course, given rise to any number of fine recipes, all of which are tantalizingly tasty and naturally light. It's awfully easy to count calories when you're working with seafood, because the numbers are so favorable. For example, one-quarter pound of uncooked shelled shrimp, a generous serving, contains only about 120 calories, compared to approximately 265 for the same amount of extra-lean raw beef. So it's not surprising that in this chapter, except for the paella, which adds up because it contains chicken and rice as well as seafood, and the grilled salmon, a naturally fatty fish, none of the recipes in this chapter is over 300 calories, and many are well below.

All kinds of seafood provide an excellent source of high-quality protein, significantly lower than red meat in saturated fat. And fish lends itself to a wide variety of preparations: grilling, baking, braising, poaching. With the proper technique, you can even "fry" fish to create a crispy coating; see Fried Catfish with Jalapeño Tartar Sauce on page 88.

Because that extra smokiness is so pleasing, and here in America, as in Mexico, we are so fond of grilling, I've included half a dozen ways to cook fish on the grill. Most of these recipes are incredibly simple and are accompanied by a zesty sauce, which you can choose to serve or not.

Especially light dishes include Grilled Shrimp with Avocado and Pink Grapefruit, a delightful main course salad, and South-of-the-Border Shrimp and Vegetable Kebabs, both of which make perfect light meals for a warm summer night.

Tomatoes, which add lots of flavor and few calories, figure in many Mexican seafood dishes. I've included Baked Snapper with Tomatoes and Herbs, Red Snapper Veracruzana and Squid Simmered with Tomatoes and Olives as several of my favorites. By the way, if you've never tried it, you should know that squid is one of the best bargains in the fish market. It is high in protein, very low in fat and calories (the recipe in this chapter comes in at an amazingly low 113 calories), mild flavored and usually quite reasonable in price.

And no collection of seafood recipes would be complete without the aforementioned Paella, the Spanish showstopper that transforms simple rice, seafood and chicken into a dish fit for a king at under 400 calories.

Baked Snapper with Tomatoes and Herbs

4 Servings   **170 Calories per serving**

Vegetable cooking spray
4 red snapper fillets (5 ounces each)
½ teaspoon salt
½ teaspoon dried oregano
½ teaspoon crushed hot red pepper
1 small onion, thinly sliced and separated into rings
1 large garlic clove, thinly sliced
2 ripe plum tomatoes, cut into ¼-inch slices
1 bay leaf, broken in half
¾ cup unsalted or reduced-sodium chicken broth, heated to boiling
¼ cup dry white wine
1½ tablespoons chopped parsley, for garnish

1. Preheat the oven to 400° F. Spray a 9 × 13-inch baking dish with vegetable cooking spray and arrange the red snapper fillets in the dish in a single layer. Season the fish with the salt, oregano and hot pepper. Arrange the onion rings, sliced garlic, sliced tomatoes and bay leaf halves over the fish and pour the hot chicken broth and the wine into the bottom of the dish.

2. Cover the dish tightly with aluminum foil and bake 10 to 12 minutes, until the fish is opaque throughout and just begins to flake when prodded with a fork. Remove the dish from the oven and transfer the fish with the tomatoes and onion rings to a serving platter. Cover with foil to keep warm.

3. Remove and discard the bay leaf pieces from the pan juices. If there is more than ½ cup juice in the pan, pour into a small nonaluminum saucepan and boil over high heat until reduced to about ½ cup. Pour the hot juice over the fish and serve, garnished with a sprinkling of parsley.

— *Fried Catfish with Jalapeño Tartar Sauce* —

A nonstick skillet and vegetable cooking spray allow calorie counters to achieve the light, pleasing crispness of fried fish without any oiliness.

6 SERVINGS   290 CALORIES PER SERVING

½ cup cornmeal, preferably stone-ground
¼ cup ground ancho chile powder
1 tablespoon ground cumin
1 tablespoon ground coriander
¾ teaspoon salt
¼ teaspoon freshly ground black pepper
6 catfish fillets (6 ounces each)
1½ tablespoons olive oil or corn oil
½ cup Jalapeño Tartar Sauce (recipe follows) or lemon wedges, as
  accompaniment

1. Preheat the oven to 400° F. In a medium bowl, combine the cornmeal, ground chile powder, cumin, coriander, salt and black pepper. Dredge the catfish fillets lightly in the seasoned cornmeal; shake off any excess.

2. Heat the oil in a large ovenproof skillet or flameproof gratin dish over medium-high heat. Add the fish and cook until golden on the bottom, 3 to 5 minutes. Turn the fillets over and cook until the second side is golden and beginning to brown, about 2 minutes.

3. Transfer the pan to the oven and bake 8 to 10 minutes, or until the cornmeal coating is lightly browned and the fish is tender and opaque throughout.

4. To serve, arrange a catfish fillet on each dinner plate and place a rounded tablespoonful of Jalapeño Tartar Sauce next to the fish.

Jalapeño Tartar Sauce

⅓ cup no-cholesterol mayonnaise
½ teaspoon Dijon mustard
2 pickled jalapeño peppers, minced
2 tablespoons sweet pickle relish, drained
¼ cup finely chopped celery
¼ cup thinly sliced scallions
2 tablespoons chopped parsley
2 teaspoons fresh lime juice
Salt and freshly ground black pepper

In a small bowl, combine the mayonnaise, mustard, pickled jalapeño peppers, pickle relish, celery, scallions, parsley and lime juice. Season with salt and pepper to taste. Mix well, cover and refrigerate at least 30 minutes before using to let flavors blend and mellow.

Grilled Salmon with Salsa Picante

4 salmon steaks (5 to 6 ounces each) or 6 portions of salmon fillet (5 to
  6 ounces each)
Juice of 2 limes
¾ teaspoon salt
¼ teaspoon freshly ground black pepper
1 tablespoon olive oil
1 cup Salsa Picante (recipe follows), as accompaniment

1. Put the salmon in a shallow dish and sprinkle on both sides with the lime juice, salt and pepper. Cover lightly with plastic wrap and let marinate at room temperature 30 minutes or refrigerate for up to 2 hours.

2. Meanwhile, light a hot fire in a grill or preheat your broiler. Brush the olive oil over the salmon and grill or broil about 4 inches from the heat, turning once, about 4 to 6 minutes per side, depending on the thickness of the pieces, until the salmon is nicely browned outside and opaque but still juicy in the center. Serve with Salsa Picante.

Salsa Picante

This zesty relish makes a savory garnish for grilled vegetables as well as fish and meats.

MAKES 2½ CUPS   10 CALORIES PER TABLESPOON

2 medium red bell peppers or 1 jar (7 ounces) roasted red peppers, drained and diced
2 cans (4 ounces each) diced green chiles, drained
6 scallions, thinly sliced
¼ cup tiny nonpareil capers, rinsed and drained, or use large capers and coarsely chop them
½ cup chopped parsley
2 teaspoons dried marjoram or oregano
2 tablespoons fresh lime juice
2 tablespoons juice from pickled jalapeño peppers
2 tablespoons extra virgin olive oil
¼ teaspoon salt

1. Roast the bell peppers: If you have a gas stove, hold the pepper with a pair of long tongs and turn it very slowly over a high flame until the pepper is totally blackened. Or broil as close to the heat as possible, turning, until charred all over, 5 to 10 minutes. Immediately put the pepper into a brown paper bag or cover with a damp towel and let stand for about 5 minutes. Rub off the charred skin and rinse under cool water. Remove and discard the stem, seeds and white ribs. Cut the roasted pepper into ¼-inch dice.

2. In a medium bowl, combine the diced roasted peppers with the green chiles, scallions, capers, parsley, marjoram, lime juice, jalapeño juice, oil and salt. Stir to mix well. Serve the salsa at room temperature.

Grilled Lime-Marinated Swordfish with Mango Salsa

4 SERVINGS   228 CALORIES PER SERVING

2 large limes, very thinly sliced
1 teaspoon salt

½ teaspoon freshly ground black pepper
½ teaspoon ground coriander
4 swordfish steaks (6 ounces each), cut about ¾ inch thick
Mango Salsa (recipe follows)

1. Arrange half the lime slices over the bottom of a 9-inch square baking dish. Sprinkle the limes with half of the salt, pepper and coriander. Arrange the swordfish in a single layer over the lime. Season the top side of the fish with the remaining salt, pepper and coriander and top with the remaining lime slices. Cover the dish and refrigerate 1 to 2 hours. Remove from the refrigerator about 30 minutes before cooking.

2. Light a hot fire in a grill or preheat your broiler. Remove the swordfish from the marinade and pat dry with paper towels. Set on an oiled rack and grill or broil about 4 inches from the heat, turning once, until lightly browned outside and opaque but still moist in the center, about 10 minutes. Remove the fish to serving plates and spoon 1 tablespoon Mango Salsa over each piece. Pass the remaining salsa separately.

Mango Salsa

MAKES 3 CUPS   34 CALORIES PER ¼ CUP

2 large ripe mangoes
½ medium cucumber, peeled, seeded and cut into ¼-inch dice
1 jar (4 ounces) roasted red peppers, drained and cut into ¼-inch dice
½ medium red onion, cut into ¼-inch dice
¼ cup chopped cilantro or parsley
1½ tablespoons fresh lime juice
1½ tablespoons juice from pickled jalapeño peppers
Pinch of salt

1. Peel the mangoes with a small, sharp knife. Cut the mango away from the large, flat pit in 2 pieces; then cut the mango from the narrow edges of the pit. Cut the mangoes into ¼-inch dice.

2. In a medium bowl, combine the mangoes, cucumber, roasted red peppers, red onion, cilantro, lime juice, pickled jalapeño juice and salt. Toss gently but thoroughly. Let the salsa stand at room temperature for 30 minutes to allow the flavors to mellow. Serve at room temperature or slightly chilled.

Red Snapper Veracruzana

This dish is an adaptation of a traditional recipe from the city of Veracruz. It is light but highly flavorful.

4 SERVINGS   250 CALORIES PER SERVING

1⅓ pounds boneless, skinless red snapper or other meaty fish fillets
Juice of 1 lime
½ teaspoon salt
1 teaspoon dried marjoram or oregano
1 tablespoon olive oil
1 medium white onion, chopped
2 garlic cloves, minced
1 can (14 ounces) Italian plum tomatoes, coarsely cut up, liquid
*   reserved*
16 small pimiento-stuffed olives, rinsed and finely chopped
1½ tablespoons capers, rinsed and drained
2 pickled jalapeño peppers, seeded and cut into thin strips
1½ tablespoons juice from pickled jalapeño peppers
½ teaspoon dried thyme
3 tablespoons chopped Italian (flat leaf) parsley
1 bay leaf
¼ teaspoon freshly ground black pepper

1. Cut the fish fillets into 4 equal portions. Lay the fish in a glass dish and sprinkle the pieces with the lime juice, salt and ½ teaspoon marjoram. Cover and refrigerate the fish 45 minutes.

2. Preheat the oven to 350° F. Heat the oil in a large nonstick skillet. Add the onion and cook over medium heat, stirring occasionally, until light golden, 5 to 6 minutes. Add the garlic and cook 2 minutes longer.

3. Add the tomatoes and the reserved liquid to the skillet, bring to a boil, reduce the heat and simmer, uncovered, 5 minutes. Add half of the olives and capers, the pickled jalapeño peppers, pickled pepper juice, remaining ½ teaspoon marjoram, thyme, 2 tablespoons of the chopped parsley, the bay leaf and black pepper. Cover the skillet and simmer 5 minutes longer.

4. Arrange the fish in a 9 × 13-inch baking dish. Pour the hot sauce over the fillets and bake, uncovered, 10 to 12 minutes, or until the fish is opaque but still moist in the center.

5. With a wide spatula, transfer the fish to a platter. Remove and discard the bay leaf. Pour the sauce over the fish and garnish with the remaining olives, capers and chopped parsley.

Shredded Crab with Pickled Vegetables

6 SERVINGS   146 CALORIES PER SERVING

2 tablespoons olive oil
1 large white onion, chopped
2 garlic cloves, minced
1 pound jumbo lump crab meat, picked over for bits of shell
3 or 4 pickled jalapeño peppers, chopped
3 medium tomatoes, chopped
3 tablespoons chopped fresh cilantro or parsley
½ teaspoon salt
¼ cup fresh lime juice
4 to 6 tablespoons juice from the pickled jalapeño peppers, to taste

1. In a medium nonstick skillet, heat the olive oil over medium-high heat. Add the onion and garlic and cook until softened, about 3 minutes. Remove the skillet from the heat and set aside.

2. Place the crab, pickled jalapeño peppers, tomatoes and cilantro in a large bowl. Scrape in the reserved onion and garlic with their cooking oil; toss well. Season with the salt, lime juice and juice from the pickled jalapeños and toss again. Let the mixture stand at room temperature for 30 minutes before serving.

— Grilled Tuna Steaks with Pineapple Relish —

4 SERVINGS   261 CALORIES PER SERVING

> 1 tablespoon olive oil
> 2 tablespoons fresh lemon juice
> 1 garlic clove, crushed through a press
> ½ teaspoon salt
> ¼ teaspoon freshly ground black pepper
> 4 tuna steaks (6 ounces each), cut ¾ to 1 inch thick
> Pineapple Relish (recipe follows)

1. In a small bowl, combine the olive oil, lemon juice, garlic, salt and pepper. Blend well. Brush the seasoned oil over both sides of the tuna steaks, cover with plastic wrap and let stand at room temperature 30 minutes.

2. Light a hot fire in a grill or preheat your broiler. Set the tuna on an oiled rack and grill or broil about 4 inches from the heat, turning once, until the steaks are just opaque throughout but still juicy, about 4 to 6 minutes per side. Serve at once, with a bowl of Pineapple Relish passed on the side.

—————— Pineapple Relish ——————

This refreshing mixture can be served as an appetizer with other salads, as a side dish or as a garnish with grilled fish, as we suggest above.

MAKES 2½ CUPS   19 CALORIES PER ¼ CUP

> 1 cup diced fresh pineapple
> ½ cup diced peeled and seeded cucumber
> ½ cup diced jicama or substitute ½ cup diced water chestnuts or raw
>   Jerusalem artichokes
> 1 large navel orange, peeled and cut into sections, or ½ cup canned
>   mandarin oranges, drained
> 2 tablespoons chopped cilantro or parsley
> 2 to 3 tablespoons fresh lime juice
> ½ teaspoon salt
> ⅛ teaspoon cayenne pepper

In a medium bowl, combine the pineapple with the cucumber, jicama, orange, cilantro, lime juice, salt and cayenne. Toss to mix. Let stand for 20 to 30 minutes to allow the flavors to blend. Serve at room temperature or slightly chilled.

— *Squid Simmered with Tomatoes and Olives* —

4 SERVINGS   170 CALORIES PER SERVING

1¼ pounds cleaned fresh or defrosted frozen squid (see Note)
1 tablespoon olive oil
1 medium onion, chopped
1 can (14 ounces) Italian plum tomatoes, with their juices
1 cup unsalted or reduced-sodium chicken broth
¼ cup pimiento-stuffed green olives, coarsely chopped
¼ teaspoon crushed hot red pepper
2 tablespoons finely chopped cilantro or parsley
1 tablespoon fresh lime juice
½ teaspoon salt
¼ teaspoon freshly ground black pepper

1. Slice the body of the squid crosswise into ½-inch rings. If using the tentacles, cut them lengthwise in half. Rinse the squid well in a colander under cold running water; drain thoroughly.

2. In a large nonaluminum saucepan or Dutch oven, heat the olive oil. Add the onion and cook over medium heat until soft and beginning to color, 3 to 5 minutes. Add the squid, tomatoes with their juices, chicken broth, olives and crushed red pepper. Heat to boiling. Reduce the heat to low and simmer, covered, 30 minutes.

3. Stir in the cilantro. Simmer, uncovered, until the squid is tender but still slightly chewy, about 10 minutes. Stir in the lime juice and season with the salt and pepper.

NOTE *If using whole, uncleaned squid, start with 2 pounds. Clean as follows: Take hold of the tentacles and gently but firmly pull the entrails from the body. Cut the tentacles off just below the eyes and reserve. Remove the thin skin from the body sacs and rinse the bodies inside and out under cold running water.*

Grilled Shrimp with Avocado and Pink Grapefruit

These shrimp are threaded onto long wooden skewers. To prevent the skewers from charring, be sure to soak them in cold water for at least 30 minutes before grilling.

4 SERVINGS   287 CALORIES PER SERVING

> *20 large shrimp (about 1¼ pounds), shelled and deveined*
> *3 tablespoons fresh lemon juice*
> *¾ teaspoon salt*
> *½ teaspoon freshly ground black pepper*
> *2 cups finely shredded romaine lettuce*
> *1 ripe avocado, peeled, seeded and quartered*
> *2 small pink grapefruit*
> *1 teaspoon sugar*
> *1½ tablespoons olive oil*

1. Thread 5 shrimp onto each of 4 wooden skewers. Sprinkle 2 tablespoons lemon juice over the shrimp and season with the salt and pepper. Cover and refrigerate while you prepare the plates.

2. Make a bed of shredded romaine lettuce on each of 4 plates, using ½ cup per serving. Cut each avocado quarter into 3 slices each and brush with the remaining lemon juice to prevent browning. Arrange 3 slices of avocado around the rim of each plate.

3. With a small sharp knife, peel off the outside skin and white pith from the grapefruit. Separate the segments of the grapefruit; peel off the skin from all but 4 of the segments. Divide the peeled grapefruit segments among the 4 plates. Squeeze the juice from the 4 remaining segments into a small bowl. Dissolve the sugar in the grapefruit juice, add 1 tablespoon olive oil and mix thoroughly.

4. Light a hot fire in a grill or preheat your broiler. Brush the remaining 1½ teaspoons oil over the skewered shrimp. Grill over the coals or broil about 4 inches from the heat, turning once, about 3 minutes on each side, or until lightly browned and opaque but not dry throughout. Place 1 skewer on top of each bed of lettuce and drizzle about 1 tablespoon dressing over each serving of shrimp.

Spicy Poached Shrimp Salad

4 SERVINGS   169 CALORIES PER SERVING

2 tablespoons white wine vinegar
¼ cup unsalted or reduced-sodium chicken broth
1 tablespoon olive oil
½ teaspoon salt
¼ teaspoon freshly ground black pepper
½ pound green beans
1 medium chayote, peeled and cut into 1 × ¼-inch strips or 1 medium
   zucchini, sliced
1 package (3 ounces) crab boil in a bag (see Note)
1 teaspoon crushed hot red pepper
1 pound extra-large shrimp (about 16 shrimp), shelled and deveined
4 plum tomatoes, cut into 6 wedges each

1. In a small bowl, whisk together the vinegar, chicken broth, olive oil, salt and pepper. Set the vinaigrette aside.

2. Bring a large saucepan of lightly salted water to a boil. Add the green beans and cook until crisp-tender and very green, 3 to 5 minutes. With a strainer or skimmer, transfer the beans to a colander and rinse under cold running water. Drain well.

3. Add the chayote strips or zucchini to the saucepan of boiling water. Cook until crisp-tender, 2 to 3 minutes. Drain in a colander and rinse under cold running water. Drain well.

4. Bring 3 quarts water to a boil in a large nonaluminum saucepan or Dutch oven. Add the bag of crab boil spices and the hot pepper. Reduce the heat to medium-low and simmer 15 minutes. Remove the spice bag and add the shrimp. Cook until the shrimp are pink. loosely curled and opaque throughout, about 3 minutes. Drain and let cool.

5. In a large bowl, combine the shrimp, green beans, chayote, tomatoes and vinaigrette. Toss lightly and serve at room temperature or lightly chilled.

NOTE *Crab boil in a bag is available in many supermarkets. If not, substitute 2 tablespoons mixed pickling spice tied in cheesecloth.*

Shrimp and Potato Omelet

Tortilla de patata is a Spanish potato omelet that is popular in Mexico as well. It is savory, but sturdy. Here beaten egg whites and seafood lighten the preparation and turn it into a very special dish—perfect for brunch or a light supper.

6 SERVINGS   168 CALORIES PER SERVING

½ pound medium red potatoes
1 tablespoon plus 2 teaspoons olive oil
1 medium onion, chopped
2 garlic cloves, minced
½ teaspoon salt
¼ teaspoon freshly ground black pepper
¾ pound small shrimp, shelled and deveined, or larger shrimp, cut into
*   ½-inch pieces*
2 plum tomatoes, cut into ½-inch dice
4 large eggs, separated
Vegetable cooking spray

1. Cook the potatoes in a medium saucepan of boiling water until tender, about 20 minutes. Drain and rinse under cold running water. Let stand until cool enough to handle. Then peel off the skins and cut the potatoes into ½-inch dice.

2. Heat 1 tablespoon olive oil in a large nonstick skillet. Add the onion and garlic and cook over medium heat until the onion is softened, about 3 minutes. Add the diced potatoes, turning often with a wide spatula, and cook until lightly browned, about 5 minutes. Season with the salt and pepper. Scrape into a medium bowl.

3. Heat the remaining 2 teaspoons oil in the skillet. Add the shrimp and cook, tossing, until pink, loosely curled and opaque in the center, 2 to 3 minutes. Transfer to the bowl with the potatoes. Add the diced tomatoes and toss. Set aside.

4. In a large bowl, beat the egg whites until they hold stiff peaks. In a separate bowl, beat the egg yolks until foamy. Add one-fourth of the beaten whites to the yolk mixture and fold in with a rubber spatula. Fold in the remaining egg whites until just a few streaks of white remain, then fold in the shrimp and potato mixture.

5. Preheat your broiler. Generously coat a 10-inch ovenproof skillet, preferably cast-iron, with vegetable cooking spray. Place over medium heat and pour in the egg mixture. Reduce the heat to low, cover and cook, shaking the pan occasionally, until the omelet is about three-fourths set but still moist and shiny on top, about 5 minutes. Place the pan under the broiler about 6 inches from the heat and broil until the omelet is set and the top is golden brown, 2 to 3 minutes. Serve hot or at room temperature.

South-of-the-Border Shrimp and Vegetable Kebabs

4 SERVINGS   176 CALORIES PER SERVING

> *Juice of 2 lemons (3 to 4 tablespoons)*
> *2 tablespoons olive oil*
> *1 tablespoon ground red chile powder or ½ teaspoon crushed hot red pepper*
> *2 garlic cloves, crushed through a press*
> *1 teaspoon ground coriander*
> *1 teaspoon ground cumin*
> *1 teaspoon dried oregano*
> *½ teaspoon salt*
> *¼ teaspoon freshly ground black pepper*
> *1 pound extra-large shrimp (about 16 shrimp), shelled and deveined*
> *½ pound small fresh mushrooms*
> *1 large red bell pepper, seeded and cut into 1-inch squares*
> *1 large red onion, cut into 1-inch squares*
> *2 small zucchini, cut into ½-inch-thick rounds*

1. In a medium bowl, combine the lemon juice, olive oil, chile powder, garlic, coriander, cumin, oregano, salt and pepper. Mix well. Add the shrimp and toss to coat. Set aside at room temperature, tossing occasionally, for 30 minutes.

2. Meanwhile, light a hot fire in a grill or preheat your broiler. Skewer the shrimp alternately with the mushrooms, red peppers, red onions and zucchini. Grill the kebabs, turning, until the shrimp are cooked through and the vegetables tender, about 7 to 10 minutes.

Paella

While quintessentially Spanish, paella is almost as popular in Mexico as it is in Spain. Often served as the star dish at large family gatherings on Sunday afternoons, it is a very special meal in a pot, perfect for a crowd.

8 SERVINGS   387 CALORIES PER SERVING

1½ tablespoons olive oil
1 large onion, chopped
3 garlic cloves, minced
1½ pounds skinless, boneless chicken breasts, trimmed of all fat and cut into 1-inch cubes
1 pound ripe tomatoes, seeded and chopped, or 1 can (16 ounces) crushed tomatoes
4 cups unsalted or reduced-sodium chicken broth
1 tablespoon paprika
½ teaspoon saffron threads
1¾ cups long-grain white rice
16 extra-large shrimp (about 1 pound), shelled and deveined
1 package (10 ounces) frozen peas, thawed
1 jar (7 ounces) diced roasted red peppers, drained
16 mussels in the shell, scrubbed and debearded, or littleneck clams, scrubbed, or use 8 mussels and 8 clams

1. Heat the oil in a large Dutch oven. Add the onion and cook over medium heat, stirring occasionally, until soft, 3 to 5 minutes. Add the garlic and cook until the onion is golden and the garlic is soft and fragrant, 2 to 3 minutes longer.

2. Add the chicken, raise the heat to medium-high and cook, stirring often, until the chicken loses its pink color and some pieces are lightly browned, 3 to 5 minutes. Add the tomatoes, chicken broth, paprika and saffron. Bring to a boil, stir in the rice and reduce the heat to medium-low. Cover and cook without stirring, 20 minutes.

3. Stir the shrimp, peas and roasted peppers into the paella. Cover and continue to cook over medium-low heat until the rice is tender, the liquid is absorbed and the shrimp are pink, loosely curled and opaque throughout, 5 to 10 minutes.

4. Meanwhile, bring ½ inch of water to a boil in a large saucepan. Add the mussels, cover tightly and steam over high heat just until they open, 3 to 5 minutes. Remove the mussels with a slotted spoon to a bowl; discard any that do not open.

5. Mound the paella on a large platter and arrange the mussels on top. Serve at once.

Mexican Shrimp with Rice and Jalapeño Peppers

4 SERVINGS   276 CALORIES PER SERVING

1 pound extra-large shrimp (about 16 shrimp), shelled and deveined
1½ tablespoons olive oil
2 small garlic cloves, minced
½ teaspoon ground cumin
1 teaspoon salt
½ teaspoon freshly ground black pepper
1 medium onion, chopped
2 fresh jalapeño or other hot green chile peppers, seeded and minced
2 cups hot cooked brown or white rice
2 medium ripe tomatoes, diced
2 tablespoons chopped cilantro or parsley
2 teaspoons chopped fresh oregano or ¾ teaspoon dried

1. Place the shrimp in a medium bowl and toss with 1 tablespoon of the oil, half the garlic, the cumin, ½ teaspoon of the salt and ¼ teaspoon of the pepper.

2. In a large nonstick skillet, cook the onion in the remaining 1½ teaspoons oil over medium-high heat until softened, about 3 minutes. Add the jalapeño peppers and the remaining garlic and cook until the garlic is softened and fragrant, about 2 minutes longer. Add the shrimp and cook, tossing often, until they are pink, loosely curled and opaque throughout, 3 to 4 minutes.

3. In a large serving bowl, toss the shrimp mixture with the hot cooked rice, tomatoes, cilantro, oregano, and remaining ½ teaspoon salt and ¼ teaspoon pepper. Serve at once.

Baked Sole Mexicana

6 S<small>ERVINGS</small>   223 C<small>ALORIES PER SERVING</small>

Vegetable cooking spray
6 pieces of fillet of sole or flounder (6 ounces each), patted dry with
  paper towels
Juice of 1 lime
1 teaspoon salt
½ teaspoon freshly ground black pepper
2 tablespoons olive oil
1 medium onion, minced
3 garlic cloves, minced
1 can (14 ounces) Italian peeled tomatoes, drained and chopped
1 bay leaf
½ teaspoon dried marjoram
3 fresh jalapeño peppers, seeded and minced
¼ cup chopped fresh parsley

1. Preheat the oven to 375° F. Coat a large baking dish with vegetable cooking spray. Arrange the fish fillets in a single layer and season with the lime juice, ½ teaspoon of the salt and ¼ teaspoon of the pepper.

2. In a large skillet, heat the olive oil. Add the onion and garlic and cook over medium-high heat until softened, about 3 minutes. Add the tomatoes, bay leaf, marjoram and jalapeño peppers. Cook until thickened, 5 to 7 minutes. Stir in 3 tablespoons of the chopped parsley and the remaining salt and pepper and cook 2 minutes.

3. Pour the sauce over the fillets and bake until the fish is cooked through and opaque throughout, 8 to 10 minutes. Sprinkle the remaining chopped parsley over the top and serve.

Shellfish Stew

This is a soupy stew, in the fashion of a French *bouillabaisse*. In slightly smaller portions, it could be served as a first-course soup.

6 SERVINGS   296 CALORIES PER SERVING

1½ tablespoons olive oil
1 cup chopped onion
2 garlic cloves, minced
1 pound extra-large shrimp (12 to 16), shelled and deveined
12 mussels, scrubbed and debearded
24 hard-shelled clams, such as littlenecks, scrubbed
3 cups clam juice
3 cups reduced-sodium chicken broth
¾ cup spaghetti sauce
1¼ cups fresh corn kernels or 1 package (10 ounces) frozen corn
¼ teaspoon dried thyme
¼ teaspoon dried oregano
⅛ teaspoon cayenne pepper (optional)
¼ teaspoon freshly ground black pepper
¼ teaspoon salt
1½ cups cooked brown or white rice
1 lime, cut into 6 wedges

1. In a large saucepan, heat the olive oil over medium-high heat. Add the onion and garlic and cook until soft, about 3 minutes. Add the shrimp and cook 3 minutes. Add the mussels, clams, clam juice, chicken broth, spaghetti sauce, corn, thyme, oregano, cayenne, black pepper and salt.

2. Bring to a boil and reduce the heat to a simmer. Simmer until the mussels and clams have opened, 6 to 8 minutes. Discard any mussels or clams that do not open.

3. Place ¼ cup of the cooked rice in each of 6 large soup bowls. Divide the seafood, broth and corn among the bowls and garnish each serving with 1 lime wedge.

Pan-Seared Scallops with Sweet Pepper and Jalapeño Sauce

4 SERVINGS   212 CALORIES PER SERVING

2 large red bell peppers
½ medium white onion, thinly sliced
2 garlic cloves
2 fresh jalapeño peppers, cut in half and seeded
2 tablespoons olive oil
½ teaspoon dried oregano
¾ teaspoon salt
½ teaspoon freshly ground black pepper
¼ cup unsalted or reduced-sodium chicken broth
1¼ pounds sea scallops

1. Preheat the oven to 350° F. Stem and seed the bell peppers and remove the white ribs inside. Cut into 2-inch pieces. In a medium bowl, toss the peppers, onion, garlic and jalapeño peppers with 1 tablespoon of the olive oil. Arrange the vegetables on a large baking sheet and season with the oregano, ¼ teaspoon salt and ¼ teaspoon pepper.

2. Bake the vegetables 25 to 30 minutes, or until soft. Remove the baking sheet from the oven and let cool 10 minutes. Scrape the roasted vegetables into a blender or food processor, add the chicken broth and purée until smooth. Set the sauce aside.

3. In a large nonstick skillet, heat the remaining 1 tablespoon oil. Add the scallops, season with the remaining salt and pepper and cook over medium-high heat until golden on the bottom, 4 to 5 minutes. Turn the scallops over and cook until lightly browned on the second side and opaque throughout, 3 to 4 minutes longer.

4. To serve, divide the hot scallops evenly among 4 dinner plates and drizzle the room temperature sauce over them. Serve at once.

— *Spicy Striped Bass with Onions and Garlic* —

In Mexico, pompano might be the fish of choice in this recipe, but pompano is rare and quite expensive up north, so I've used striped bass. If pompano is fresh in your market, by all means try it; red snapper also takes well to this tasty preparation.

4 SERVINGS   254 CALORIES PER SERVING

> *4 striped bass fillets (6 ounces each), skin on*
> *2½ tablespoons olive oil*
> *¾ teaspoon salt*
> *½ teaspoon freshly ground black pepper*
> *1 medium white onion, thinly sliced*
> *3 garlic cloves, minced*
> *2 fresh jalapeño peppers, seeded and minced*
> *¼ to ½ teaspoon crushed hot red pepper, to taste*

1. Brush the fish lightly on *both* sides with 1½ teaspoons of the olive oil and season with the salt and pepper.

2. Heat 1 tablespoon of the oil in a large nonstick skillet. Add the onion and cook over medium-high heat until softened, about 3 minutes. Add the garlic and cook until softened and fragrant, 1 to 2 minutes. Add the fresh jalapeño peppers and the hot pepper and cook 1 minute longer. The onion and garlic should be golden. With a rubber spatula, scrape the mixture into a small bowl and set aside.

3. Heat the remaining 1 tablespoon oil in the skillet. Add the striped bass fillets, skin side up, and cook over medium-high heat, 3 to 4 minutes, until lightly browned on the bottom. Carefully turn the fish over with a wide spatula and cook until the skin is lightly browned and the fish is opaque and white throughout but still moist, 4 to 5 minutes longer. (Note: When you turn the fish, the heat of the skillet may shrink the skin and make the fish buckle in the middle. Flatten the fillets by pressing on each with the back of a metal spatula for about 30 seconds.)

4. To serve, place each fillet, skin side down, in the center of a plate, and top with one-fourth of the onion-garlic-chile mixture.

Chapter Five

CHICKEN AND
ALL THE
OTHER MEATS

In Mexico, poultry and meats are often marinated and grilled or braised in the oven or stewed, both to add extra flavor and to tenderize them. While our chickens on the whole are younger and our cuts of red meat more tender to begin with, the recipes are no less appropriate for lighter eating. I've simply adapted them by choosing the leanest cuts available, minimizing fat and adjusting the cooking times where necessary.

Of all the meats available in Mexico, chicken is the top choice and apparently has been ever since the bird was introduced by the Spaniards in the 1500s. In fact, Latin America was ahead of us in appreciating the qualities of the bird, treating it with the respect it deserves as a special dish worthy of the big Sunday family feast, while we were still gorging ourselves on roast beef. To lighten the low-calorie meat even further, I've chosen to work with the white meat breast, usually skinless and boneless, which offers built-in portion control as well as low fat and delicious taste. Barbecued Chicken in Adobo Sauce and Orange-Marinated Chicken, flavored with citrus juice, hot peppers and herbs are just a couple of the selections.

Turkey was domesticated by the Aztecs long before the Spanish arrived in the New World, and the bird still raised in Mexico today is closer in size and shape to our wild turkey than to the plump domesticated variety sold in supermarkets in the United States. Turkey is almost as low in calories as chicken, and it is certainly as adaptable. Both Spinach-Stuffed

Turkey Cutlets and Roast Chile-Rubbed Turkey Breast take advantage of white meat turkey's special combination of rich flavor and low fat.

As for beef and pork, there is a wide range of recipes included here, from Grilled Beef Tenderloin Kebabs, loaded with chunks of lean, tender meat and lots of assorted vegetables, and Grilled Flank Steak with Black and White Chili Beans to Pork Stew with Roasted Tomatoes, Corn and Squash and Roast Pork Tenderloin with spicy Salsa Bruja. I've also included typical Mexican stews, such as Lamb and Red Chile Stew Jalisco and Rabbit Stew with Vegetables. Rabbit is one of the leanest meats available; lamb will pass muster if it's carefully trimmed and portion controlled. All of the recipes in this chapter contain under 400 calories per serving.

Baked Spiced Chicken with Corn Crust

6 SERVINGS   204 CALORIES PER SERVING

1½ pounds skinless, boneless chicken breast halves
1½ teaspoons salt
1 teaspoon ground cumin
¼ teaspoon ground allspice
¼ teaspoon ground cinnamon
¼ teaspoon cayenne pepper
Vegetable cooking spray
1 large onion, finely chopped
4 garlic cloves, thinly sliced
5 plum tomatoes, peeled and diced
10 pimiento-stuffed olives, coarsely chopped
1½ cups corn kernels—fresh, canned or thawed frozen
½ teaspoon dried oregano
1 whole egg
1 egg white

1. Preheat the oven to 375° F. Trim any visible fat from the chicken and cut the meat into 1-inch cubes. In a medium bowl, combine 1 teaspoon of the salt, the cumin, allspice, cinnamon and cayenne. Add the chicken and toss to coat.

2. Meanwhile, coat a large nonstick skillet with vegetable cooking spray and place over medium heat. Add the chicken and cook, tossing, until no longer pink on the outside, about 5 minutes. With a slotted spoon, transfer to a plate. Add the onion and cook until soft and beginning to color, about 5 minutes. Add the garlic and cook, stirring often, until the onion is golden and the garlic is soft and fragrant, about 3 minutes longer. Add the tomatoes and olives, reduce the heat to medium-low and simmer 10 minutes. Remove from the heat and add the chicken along with any juices that have collected on the plate.

3. In a blender or food processor, combine 1 cup of the corn, the oregano, whole egg, egg white and remaining ½ teaspoon salt. Purée until smooth. Transfer to a bowl and stir in the remaining ½ cup corn.

4. Coat a 2-quart soufflé dish with the cooking spray. Add the chicken in sauce and ladle the corn mixture over it. Bake until the corn crust is set and golden brown, about 25 minutes. Serve at once.

Seven-Layer Chicken Taco Salad

Actually, there is no taco in this salad, but there are all the fillings. Festive and flavorful, it is a meal in a bowl. For an extra-texture treat, serve with a basket of Crispy Corn Tostadas (p. 28) or your favorite packaged tostadas.

6 Servings   332 Calories per serving

> 1 pound skinless, boneless chicken breasts
> 2 cups unsalted or reduced-sodium chicken broth
> 3 tablespoons chopped parsley
> 3/4 teaspoon salt
> 1/2 teaspoon freshly ground black pepper
> 3 cups shredded iceberg or romaine lettuce
> 1 pound ripe tomatoes, diced
> 1 can (16 ounces) black beans, rinsed and drained
> 1 large avocado, diced
> 1 cup finely diced red onion
> 1 cup shredded reduced-fat Monterey Jack cheese (4 ounces)
> 3 tablespoons cider vinegar
> 2 tablespoons olive oil

1. Trim any visible fat from the chicken breasts, rinse them under cold running water and place in a medium saucepan. Add the chicken broth and enough water to cover by 2 inches. Bring to a simmer over medium-high heat, reduce the heat to medium-low and cook until the chicken is white throughout with no trace of pink in the center but still moist, 10 to 15 minutes. Let the chicken remain in the liquid until cool enough to handle, about 20 minutes.

2. Remove the chicken from the broth and tear into shreds. Reserve 1/3 cup of the broth. In a small bowl, toss the shredded chicken with the parsley, 1/2 teaspoon of the salt and 1/4 teaspoon of the pepper.

3. In a wide shallow bowl, layer the lettuce, tomatoes, black beans, chicken and avocado. Scatter the red onion over the avocado and sprinkle the cheese around the inside of the bowl in a wide ring.

4. In a small bowl, whisk together the vinegar, olive oil and remaining 1/4 teaspoon each salt and pepper with the reserved 1/3 cup chicken broth. Drizzle the dressing over the salad and serve.

Chicken and Vegetable Salad

Filled with vegetables and shredded chicken, this delicious salad is a complete low-calorie lunch or light supper.

4 SERVINGS   292 CALORIES PER SERVING

¾ pound skinless, boneless chicken breasts
½ pound red potatoes, scrubbed and cut into ½-inch dice
2 medium carrots, peeled and sliced
½ cup frozen peas, thawed
3 tablespoons olive oil
1 medium white onion, thinly sliced
4 large mushrooms, sliced
2 tablespoons white wine vinegar
½ teaspoon salt
¼ teaspoon freshly ground black pepper
1 small head of romaine lettuce, trimmed and cut crosswise into ½-
* inch-wide strips*
Wedges of tomato and chopped parsley, for garnish

1. Put the chicken in a medium saucepan of lightly salted water. Bring to a simmer over medium-high heat, reduce the heat to medium-low and cook until the chicken is white throughout with no trace of pink in the center but still moist, 10 to 15 minutes. Remove the pan from the heat and let the chicken remain in the liquid until cool enough to handle. Remove the chicken and tear or cut into ½-inch strips. Reserve ¼ cup of the liquid.

2. Meanwhile, bring another medium saucepan of salted water to a boil. Add the potatoes and carrots. Return to a boil and cook until the vegetables are tender but still firm, 6 to 8 minutes. Add the peas and drain immediately into a colander. Rinse under cold running water; drain well.

3. Heat 1 tablespoon of the oil in a large nonstick skillet. Add the onion and cook over medium-high heat 2 minutes. Add the mushrooms and cook, stirring often, until the onions and mushrooms are tender and any liquid from the mushrooms has evaporated, about 5 minutes.

4. In a medium bowl, whisk together the vinegar, salt, pepper, remaining 2 tablespoons olive oil and reserved ¼ cup broth. Add the shredded chicken, potatoes, carrots, peas, onion and mushrooms. Toss to coat.

5. Place the lettuce on a platter or divide among 4 plates and mound the chicken and vegetable salad on top. Garnish with tomato wedges and chopped parsley. Serve at room temperature or slightly chilled.

Quick and Easy Chicken Tamales

In Mexico, tamales are usually wrapped for steaming in either corn husks or banana leaves. Aluminum foil makes a convenient substitute.

4 SERVINGS   258 CALORIES PER SERVING

> *¾ pound skinless, boneless chicken breasts*
> *4 cups unsalted or reduced-sodium chicken broth or water*
> *Vegetable cooking spray*
> *1 small onion, cut into slivers*
> *1 large garlic clove, minced*
> *½ teaspoon dried marjoram*
> *¼ teaspoon ground cumin*
> *¾ teaspoon salt*
> *½ teaspoon freshly ground black pepper*
> *1 cup yellow cornmeal, preferably stone-ground*

1. Trim off any visible fat on the chicken. Rinse under cold running water. Place in a medium saucepan with the broth and bring to a simmer over medium-high heat. Reduce the heat to medium-low and simmer until the chicken is white throughout with no trace of pink in the center, but still moist, 10 to 15 minutes. Remove the pan from the heat and let stand in the broth until cool enough to handle. Tear the chicken into thin strips. Strain and reserve the broth.

2. Coat a small nonstick skillet with vegetable cooking spray. Add the onion and cook over medium heat, stirring occasionally, until soft, about 3 minutes. Add the garlic and cook until soft and fragrant, about 2 minutes longer. Add the marjoram, cumin, ¼ teaspoon of the salt and ¼ teaspoon of the black pepper and cook 1 minute, stirring constantly. Remove the skillet from the heat, add the shredded chicken and toss. Set the chicken filling aside.

3. In a medium bowl, whisk together the cornmeal and 1 cup of the reserved broth. Pour into a medium saucepan and slowly whisk in 2 more cups of the broth. Add the remaining ½ teaspoon salt and ¼ teaspoon pepper. Place the saucepan over medium heat and cook, stirring constantly with a wooden spoon, until the cornmeal is very thick, about 5 minutes. Remove from the heat and let cool slightly.

4. Tear off 12 sheets of aluminum foil, each about 9 × 12 inches. Scoop

about ¼ cup of the cornmeal onto each piece of foil. Spread into a 2 × 4-inch rectangle. Spoon 2 tablespoons of the chicken filling down the center of the dough. Fold up the long sides of the foil so the edges meet, lifting the cornmeal to enclose the chicken in the center. Fold the edges of the foil over twice to seal and wrap the foil snugly around the tamales.

5. Place the tamales in a steamer or on a rack in a saucepan over boiling water, cover and steam until the dough is cooked through, about 20 minutes. Serve the tamales in their foil, and let your guests unwrap them as they eat. Allow 3 tamales per person.

Roasted Garlic Chicken with Potatoes

6 SERVINGS   304 CALORIES PER SERVING

1½ tablespoons olive oil
1 whole roasting chicken (3½ to 4 pounds), skin removed, cut into
   serving pieces
1 teaspoon salt
½ teaspoon freshly ground black pepper
1 medium onion, chopped
12 garlic cloves, peeled
12 small white or red potatoes, cut into quarters
¼ cup cider vinegar
3 cups reduced-sodium chicken broth
1 bay leaf
½ teaspoon dried thyme
½ teaspoon dried marjoram

1. In a large, heavy flameproof casserole with a lid, heat the olive oil over medium-high heat. Season the chicken with ½ teaspoon of the salt and ¼ teaspoon of the pepper and add to the pan. Cook, turning, until browned on both sides, about 10 minutes. As the pieces brown, remove them to a plate and reserve. Add the onion and the garlic to the pan and cook them in the same oil as the chicken until lightly browned, 3 to 5 minutes. Add the potatoes and cook, stirring frequently, for 5 minutes. Return the chicken and any juices that may have accumulated on the plate to the casserole.

2. Add the vinegar, chicken broth, bay leaf, thyme, marjoram and the remaining ½ teaspoon salt and ¼ teaspoon pepper. Cover and cook until the chicken is tender, about 45 minutes.

Spinach-Stuffed Turkey Cutlets

Turkey is both New World in origin and extremely low in calories, which makes it the perfect meat for light Mexican cooking.

8 SERVINGS   176 CALORIES PER SERVING

> *8 uncooked turkey cutlets (4 ounces each)*
> *1½ teaspoons salt*
> *½ teaspoon freshly ground black pepper*
> *1 small onion, chopped*
> *2 garlic cloves, minced*
> *1 tablespoon olive oil*
> *½ teaspoon ground cumin*
> *⅛ teaspoon cayenne pepper*
> *1 small zucchini, cut into ½-inch dice*
> *½ cup corn kernels—fresh, canned or thawed frozen*
> *1 can (4 ounces) diced green chiles, drained*
> *1 jar (4 ounces) diced roasted red peppers, drained*
> *1 package (10 ounces) frozen chopped spinach, thawed and squeezed*
>   *dry*
> *Vegetable cooking spray*

1. Preheat the oven to 350° F. Pound the turkey cutlets between two sheets of wax paper until evenly flattened to about ¼ inch. Season the turkey on both sides with 1 teaspoon salt and the pepper and arrange in a single layer on 2 baking sheets.

2. In a large nonstick skillet, cook the onion and garlic in the olive oil over medium heat until the onion is soft, about 3 minutes. Add the cumin and cayenne and cook, stirring, 1 minute longer. Add the zucchini and cook, stirring often, until crisp-tender, 3 to 4 minutes. Add the corn, green chiles, roasted red peppers, spinach, and remaining ½ teaspoon salt. Cook until the vegetables are all heated through and the spinach is tender, 3 to 5 minutes.

3. Coat a 9 × 13-inch baking dish with vegetable cooking spray. Spoon about ¼ cup of the vegetable filling onto each turkey cutlet. Roll up to enclose the filling and arrange, seam side down, in the baking dish. Bake 20 to 25 minutes, until the turkey is tender and white throughout.

Roast Chile-Rubbed Turkey Breast

8 to 10 Servings   309 Calories per serving

1 turkey breast (about 6 pounds)
1 medium onion, cut into quarters
2 garlic cloves, crushed through a press
2 tablespoons olive oil
2 tablespoons frozen orange juice concentrate
3 tablespoons ground red chile powder or 2 tablespoons chili powder
1 teaspoon salt
1 teaspoon dried oregano
½ teaspoon ground cumin
½ teaspoon ground coriander
¼ teaspoon freshly ground black pepper

1. Remove the turkey breast from the refrigerator 30 minutes before cooking. Remove the skin and trim off any visible fat.

2. In a food processor or blender, combine the onion, garlic, olive oil, orange juice, chile powder, salt, oregano, cumin, coriander and black pepper. Purée until smooth. Rub this seasoning mixture all over the turkey breast.

3. Preheat the oven to 325° F. Place the turkey breast in a small roasting pan and cover with aluminum foil. Roast the breast 45 minutes, uncover and roast 30 minutes longer, or until the juices run clear from the thickest part of the breast when pierced with a skewer; an instant-reading thermometer should register 170° F.

4. Transfer the turkey breast to a carving board, cover loosely with the foil and let stand 5 to 10 minutes before carving into thin slices.

Chili with Pinto Beans

6 SERVINGS   233 CALORIES PER SERVING

2 teaspoons olive oil
1 medium onion, chopped
2 medium celery ribs, chopped
2 garlic cloves, minced
1 pound ground sirloin (90% lean)
1½ tablespoons chili powder
1 teaspoon ground cumin
1 teaspoon dried oregano
½ teaspoon crushed hot red pepper, or to taste
1 can (28 ounces) Italian plum tomatoes, with their juices
1 tablespoon Worcestershire sauce
2 teaspoons cider vinegar
1 bay leaf
1 teaspoon salt
½ teaspoon freshly ground black pepper
1 can (16 ounces) pinto beans, drained and rinsed
Optional garnishes:
Diced white onion—4 calories per tablespoon
Shredded reduced-fat Cheddar—23 calories per tablespoon
Low-fat yogurt or nonfat sour cream—9 and 10 calories per
   tablespoon, respectively
Sliced pickled jalapeño peppers—2 calories per tablespoon
Sliced black olives—10 calories per tablespoon

1. Heat the oil in a large nonstick skillet or Dutch oven. Add the onion and celery and cook over medium heat until the vegetables are softened and the onion is just beginning to color, 5 to 7 minutes. Add the garlic and cook, stirring often, until the garlic is soft and fragrant and the onion is golden, 2 to 3 minutes longer.

2. Crumble the beef into the skillet and cook, stirring to break up any lumps of meat, until the beef is no longer pink, 5 to 7 minutes. Add the chili powder, cumin, oregano and hot pepper. Cook, stirring, 1 to 2 minutes to toast the spices. Add the tomatoes with their juices, the Worcestershire, cider vinegar, bay leaf, salt and pepper. Bring to a boil, stirring and breaking up the tomatoes with the side of a large spoon. Reduce the heat to medium-low and simmer, partially covered, until the chili is thickened, 20 to 25 minutes.

3. Add the beans and simmer 10 minutes longer. Remove and discard the bay leaf. To serve, set out the garnishes separately on the table so guests can help themselves. Ladle the chili into bowls.

Grilled Beef Tenderloin Kebabs

Tenderloin, or fillet, is the leanest part of the beef; it cooks quickly and is best done rare. If you prefer, you can substitute sirloin, but assume the calorie count will be somewhat higher.

4 SERVINGS   323 CALORIES PER SERVING

1¼ pounds beef tenderloin, trimmed of all fat, cut into 1½-inch cubes
1½ tablespoons fresh lime juice
1 tablespoon olive oil
1 teaspoon dried oregano
¾ teaspoon salt
½ teaspoon freshly ground black pepper
1 large red onion, cut into 1½-inch pieces
1 large green bell pepper, stemmed, seeded and cut into 1½-inch pieces
1 cup Chipotle Tomato Sauce (p. 59)

1. In a small bowl, toss the beef cubes with the lime juice, olive oil, oregano, salt and pepper. Thread the beef alternately with the red onion and green pepper onto long metal skewers.

2. Light a hot fire in a grill or preheat your broiler. Set the skewers on the grill rack or under the broiler about 4 inches from the heat. Grill or broil, 2 to 3 minutes per side, turning, until the meat is browned outside but rare inside and the vegetables are just tender and lightly browned.

3. Serve the skewers on a platter or slide the meat and vegetables off each skewer onto 4 dinner plates. Drizzle ¼ cup of the Chipotle Tomato Sauce over each serving.

Beefy Tamale Pie

6 SERVINGS   364 CALORIES PER SERVING

Vegetable cooking spray
1 medium white onion, chopped
2 small garlic cloves, minced
1½ pounds ground sirloin (90% lean)
1 teaspoon dried oregano
¼ to ½ teaspoon crushed hot red pepper, to taste
½ teaspoon ground cumin
1 can (16 ounces) pinto beans, drained and rinsed
1 can (16 ounces) canned crushed tomatoes
½ cup corn kernels
¾ teaspoon salt
⅜ teaspoon freshly ground black pepper
¾ cup yellow cornmeal
½ cup grated reduced-fat Muenster cheese

1. Coat a large nonstick skillet with vegetable cooking spray. Add the onion and cook over medium heat, stirring often, until the onion is beginning to color, about 5 minutes. Add the garlic and cook 1 minute longer. Crumble the beef into the skillet. Continue to cook over medium heat, stirring to break up any lumps of meat, until the onion is lightly browned and the meat no longer pink, about 5 minutes.

2. Add the oregano, hot pepper and cumin and cook, stirring, 1 minute. Add the pinto beans, tomatoes, corn, ½ teaspoon of the salt and ¼ teaspoon of the pepper. Reduce the heat to medium-low and simmer, uncovered and stirring occasionally, until thickened, about 15 minutes. Remove from the heat and set aside.

3. In a medium saucepan, bring 1½ cups water to a boil. In a medium heat-proof bowl, combine the cornmeal with the remaining ¼ teaspoon salt and ⅛ teaspoon pepper. Gradually whisk in ½ cup cold water until smooth. Slowly stir the wetted cornmeal into the boiling water. Cook over medium heat, stirring constantly, until the cornmeal is almost tender and the mixture is quite thick, 3 to 5 minutes.

4. Preheat the oven to 350° F. Lightly coat a 9-inch square baking dish with the cooking spray. Spoon the beef mixture into the dish. Top with the cooked cornmeal and spread evenly to cover. Sprinkle the cheese evenly over the top. Bake until the cornmeal crust is set and dry throughout, the cheese is golden brown and the casserole is very hot at the center, 30 to 40 minutes.

Beef Stew with Vegetables

6 SERVINGS   260 CALORIES PER SERVING

1½ pounds well-trimmed beef chuck, cut into 1-inch cubes
1 medium white onion, chopped
4 garlic cloves, finely chopped
1 bay leaf
1 teaspoon dried marjoram or oregano
1 teaspoon dried thyme
½ teaspoon salt
¼ teaspoon freshly ground black pepper
1 can (13½ ounces) beef broth
6 small boiling potatoes (about ¾ pound), cut in half
3 medium carrots, peeled and sliced into ¼-inch-thick rounds
2 ears of corn, husks and silk removed, cut crosswise into 1-inch rounds
2 medium zucchini, thickly sliced
⅓ cup thinly sliced scallions
2 tablespoons minced jalapeño or other fresh hot green chile peppers, or
   less to taste

1. In a large saucepan or Dutch oven, combine the beef, onion, garlic, bay leaf, marjoram, thyme, salt, pepper and beef broth. Add enough cold water to barely cover the ingredients. Heat to boiling, reduce the heat to medium-low, cover and simmer, skimming off any fat or scum that rises to the surface, 1½ hours.

2. Add the potatoes and carrots; if necessary, add a little more water. Cover and simmer 20 minutes. Add the corn and zucchini and simmer until the beef and all the vegetables are tender, about 10 minutes longer. Season with additional salt and pepper to taste. Remove and discard the bay leaf.

3. To serve, ladle the stew into serving bowls, dividing the meat and vegetables evenly and giving everyone some of the broth; it is a soupy stew. Garnish each portion with 1 tablespoon sliced scallions and 1 teaspoon minced jalapeños.

Pork Stew with Roasted Tomatoes, Corn and Squash

Corn, squash and tomatoes are all vegetables that the Spanish discovered when they arrived in South America. Lucky for dieters because a variety of vegetables are the best way to stretch quantity and still keep calories down.

6 SERVINGS   304 CALORIES PER SERVING

> *7 ripe plum tomatoes*
> *1 medium onion, sliced ½ inch thick*
> *3 garlic cloves*
> *2 tablespoons olive oil*
> *1 teaspoon salt*
> *½ teaspoon freshly ground black pepper*
> *3 dried ancho chiles (about 2 ounces)*
> *1½ cups boiling water*
> *1½ pounds well-trimmed boneless pork loin, cut into 1-inch cubes*
> *2 chayote squash or medium zucchini, cut into 2 × ½-inch strips*
> *1 cup corn kernels—fresh, canned or thawed frozen*
> *1 medium red bell pepper, roasted (p. 150), or 1 jar (4 ounces) roasted*
> *   red peppers, cut into thin strips*

1. Preheat the oven to 400° F. Arrange the tomatoes, onion and garlic in a small roasting pan or on a baking sheet and brush both sides of the onion slices with 1½ teaspoons of the oil. Roast until the vegetables begin to brown, 10 to 12 minutes. Turn and bake until the tomato skins are split and the onion and garlic are lightly browned, 8 to 10 minutes longer. Remove from the oven and let cool.

2. Remove the stems from the chiles and tap out the seeds. Tear the chiles into 2-inch pieces and place in a medium heatproof bowl. Pour the boiling water over the chiles and let stand until they have softened, about 30 minutes. Put the chiles and the liquid into a food processor along with the salt and pepper. Purée until smooth. Scrape into a bowl and set the chile purée aside. There is no need to rinse the blender.

3. Peel the tomatoes and put them into the food processor along with the onion slices and garlic. Pulse several times, until the vegetables are coarsely chopped. Set aside.

4. In a large Dutch oven, heat the remaining 1½ tablespoons oil. Add the pork cubes and cook over medium-high heat, turning, until browned all over, about 5 minutes. Remove the pork with a slotted spoon and drain the

browned pork on paper towels. Pour off any fat from the pan and carefully wipe it out with paper towels.

5. Return the pork to the Dutch oven. Add the chile purée and chopped roasted vegetables and simmer over medium-low heat, partially covered and stirring occasionally, until the pork is tender and the sauce is thickened, about 45 minutes. Add the squash and simmer, uncovered, 5 minutes. Add the corn and roasted pepper strips and simmer 5 minutes longer. Ladle into bowls to serve.

Pozole

8 SERVINGS   348 CALORIES PER SERVING

1 tablespoon olive oil
1 pound boneless pork loin, trimmed and cut into 1-inch cubes
1 pound skinless, boneless chicken breasts, cut into 1-inch pieces
2 medium onions, chopped
4 garlic cloves, minced
1 teaspoon dried marjoram or oregano
1 teaspoon dried basil
2 bay leaves
1 small smoked ham hock (about 6 ounces)
2 cans (27 ounces) white hominy, rinsed and drained
1 teaspoon freshly ground black pepper
Shredded green cabbage and thinly sliced radishes, for garnish

1. In a large Dutch oven, heat the olive oil over medium-high heat. Add the pork and cook, turning, until browned all over, about 5 minutes. With a slotted spoon, remove the pork to a plate. Add the chicken pieces and cook, turning, until lightly browned, about 3 minutes. Remove to the plate.

2. Add the onions to the pan, reduce the heat to medium and cook, stirring occasionally, until the onions start to brown, about 5 minutes. Add the garlic and cook, stirring often, until tender and fragrant, about 2 minutes longer. Add the marjoram, basil and bay leaves and the ham hock. Return the pork and chicken to the pan, along with any juices that have collected on the plate.

3. Add enough water to barely cover the ingredients. Bring to a boil over high heat, reduce the heat to medium-low and simmer, partially covered, 1 hour. Remove and discard the bay leaf. Add the hominy and simmer 15 minutes longer. Season with the pepper and ladle into bowls; this is a soupy stew. Garnish each portion with a little shredded cabbage and a sprinkling of radishes. Serve at once.

Orange-Marinated Chicken

Grilling is a great way to impart flavor with no added fat. While outdoor grills are popular, they can be limiting if you live in a northern state, and broiling doesn't give any of that tantalizing smoky taste. Cast-iron grill pans are a wonderful alternative, and an excellent investment if you are dieting. They are inexpensive, quick-cooking and remarkably effective. And because they are ridged, any exuded fat drains right off. Alternatively the chicken can be grilled outside or broiled, in which case the cooking time will be several minutes longer.

6 SERVINGS   156 CALORIES PER SERVING

> *2 seedless oranges, cut in half and each half cut into quarters*
> *1 medium onion, cut in half and each half cut into quarters*
> *1 can (7 ounces) chipotle peppers in adobo sauce*
> *3 garlic cloves*
> *⅓ cup chopped cilantro or parsley*
> *2 tablespoons olive oil*
> *1 teaspoon dried marjoram or oregano*
> *¾ teaspoon dried thyme*
> *1 teaspoon salt*
> *6 skinless, boneless chicken breasts (4 ounces each), trimmed of all fat and pounded to a thickness of ½ inch*
> *¼ teaspoon freshly ground black pepper*
> *Vegetable cooking spray*

1. In a food processor, combine the oranges, onion, chipotle peppers and sauce, garlic, cilantro, olive oil, marjoram, thyme and ½ teaspoon salt. Process until all is finely chopped.

2. Pour half the marinade into the bottom of a nonaluminum pan large enough to hold the chicken breasts in one layer. Arrange the chicken in the pan and pour the rest of the marinade over the chicken. Cover with plastic wrap and marinate the chicken in the refrigerator 12 to 24 hours. Wipe the marinade from the chicken and season with the remaining ½ teaspoon salt and the black pepper.

3. Coat a cast-iron grill pan with vegetable cooking spray. Heat over high heat until a drop of water sizzles upon contact, about 3 minutes. Reduce the heat to medium-high, add the chicken breasts and cook until nicely browned on one side, 3 to 5 minutes. If you like, rotate the chicken 45 degrees about halfway through so you'll get those pretty crisscross grill marks. Turn the chicken over and cook until the chicken is browned on the bottom and white throughout with no trace of pink in the center but still juicy, 4 to 5 minutes.

Barbecued Chicken in Adobo Sauce

6 SERVINGS   165 CALORIES PER SERVING

> *6 chicken breast halves on the bone (about 3½ pounds total)*
> *Adobo Sauce (recipe follows)*
> *2 cups shredded romaine lettuce*
> *2 ripe plum tomatoes, diced*
> *1 bunch of radishes, thinly sliced*

1. Remove the skin from the chicken breasts, rinse under cold running water and pat dry with paper towels. Place the chicken in a shallow dish and rub 1 cup of the Adobo Sauce generously over both sides. Let the chicken marinate, covered, at room temperature up to 1 hour or in the refrigerator up to 24 hours.

2. Light a medium fire in a grill or preheat your broiler. Remove the chicken from the marinade; discard the marinade. Grill the chicken breasts or broil about 6 inches from the heat, turning several times, until no trace of pink remains at the center of the thickest parts, about 20 minutes.

3. Meanwhile, make a bed of the shredded romaine lettuce in the center of a serving platter. Top with the tomatoes and radishes. To serve, arrange the grilled chicken around the vegetables and drizzle a little of the sauce over the meat. Serve the chicken hot or at room temperature, with the remaining adobo sauce passed separately on the side.

Adobo Sauce

6 dried ancho chiles (about 4 ounces)
2 cups boiling water
1 tablespoon olive oil
1½ medium onions, diced (about 2 cups)
4 large garlic cloves, chopped
2 tablespoons red wine vinegar
3 tablespoons firmly packed brown sugar
1 bay leaf
½ teaspoon dried thyme
½ teaspoon dried oregano
½ teaspoon ground cumin
½ teaspoon freshly ground black pepper
¼ teaspoon ground cinnamon

1. Preheat the oven to 375° F. Remove the stems from the chiles and tap out the seeds. Toast on a baking sheet about 6 minutes. Remove from the oven, let cool, then tear the chiles into 2-inch pieces and place in a heatproof bowl. Pour the boiling water over the chiles and let stand until softened, about 30 minutes.

2. Heat the olive oil in a large nonaluminum saucepan over medium heat. Add the onions and cook until light brown, 6 to 7 minutes. Add the garlic and cook 1 minute longer. Add the chiles and their liquid, the wine vinegar, brown sugar, bay leaf, thyme, oregano, cumin, black pepper and cinnamon. Heat to simmering, reduce the heat to low, cover and cook 15 minutes. Let cool slightly. Remove and discard the bay leaf.

3. Transfer the mixture to a blender or food processor and purée until smooth. The sauce will be thick; add 2 to 3 tablespoons water if the purée is too thick. Let cool to room temperature before using.

Roast Pork Tenderloin with Salsa Bruja

Pork tenderloin, the thin strip of lean meat that lies along the rib, is the leanest cut of the pig, but hard to come by in some markets. If tenderloin is not available, use an equal weight of center-cut loin, but be sure to increase the cooking time as described below.

6 SERVINGS   196 CALORIES PER SERVING

> 1 tablespoon olive oil
> 1 tablespoon ground red chile powder, preferably ancho
> 1 teaspoon ground cumin
> 1 teaspoon salt
> ⅛ teaspoon freshly ground black pepper
> 2 pounds pork tenderloin or center-cut boneless pork loin, trimmed of
>   all visible fat
> Vegetable cooking spray
> Salsa Bruja (recipe follows)

1. In a medium bowl, combine the olive oil, chile powder, cumin, salt and pepper. Put the meat into the bowl and rub all over with the oil and seasonings. Cover the bowl and marinate the meat at room temperature 30 minutes.

2. Preheat the oven to 400° F. Coat an ovenproof skillet or flameproof gratin dish with vegetable cooking spray and heat over medium-high heat. Add the pork and cook, turning, until lightly browned all over, 6 to 8 minutes. Transfer to the oven and roast 20 minutes for the tenderloin or 45 minutes for the loin, or until the meat is white throughout with no trace of pink in the center, but is still moist. Carve the pork into ¼-inch slices and serve with Salsa Bruja or a milder salsa, if you prefer.

Salsa Bruja

MAKES 1½ CUPS   28 CALORIES PER ¼ CUP

> *3 large tomatoes*
> *5 fresh jalapeño peppers*
> *½ head of garlic, cut in half crosswise*
> *½ teaspoon salt*

1. Preheat your broiler. Arrange the tomatoes and jalapeño peppers on a baking sheet. Place the garlic on the sheet, cut sides up. Broil about 4 inches from the heat until the vegetables are browned on one side. Turn and brown on other side. Remove the baking sheet from the broiler and cover tightly with foil. Let cool about 20 minutes.

2. Peel the tomatoes and peppers; seed the peppers unless you want the sauce even spicier. Squeeze the garlic cloves from their skins. Put the vegetables and salt into a blender or food processor and purée until fairly smooth. Pour into a bowl and serve at room temperature.

Pork Loin in Red Chile Sauce with Pineapple and Peaches

Pork is 50 percent leaner than it was 20 years ago. The leanest cuts, the loin and tenderloin, have less than 5 grams of fat and 166 calories in a 3½-ounce serving. This equals skinless white meat chicken in both calorie and fat content.

8 SERVINGS   311 CALORIES PER SERVING

> *8 medium dried ancho chiles (about 6 ounces)*
> *4 cups boiling water*
> *½ cup dry-roasted peanuts*
> *1½ teaspoons salt*
> *½ teaspoon freshly ground black pepper*

½ teaspoon ground cinnamon
⅛ teaspoon ground cloves
1 tablespoon olive oil
2 pounds boneless pork loin, trimmed and cut into 1-inch cubes
1 large white onion, chopped
5 large garlic cloves, minced
2 cups unsalted or reduced-sodium chicken broth
¼ cup frozen orange juice concentrate
2 tablespoons cider vinegar
1½ cups cubed fresh pineapple
1½ cups sliced peaches—fresh, frozen or canned, drained

1. Remove the stems from the chiles and tap out the seeds. Tear the chiles into large pieces; place in a medium heatproof bowl and cover with the boiling water. Let stand 30 minutes, or until very soft. Purée the chiles with 2 cups of the soaking liquid in a blender or food processor. Set the chile purée aside.

2. Meanwhile, in a food processor, combine the peanuts, salt, pepper, cinnamon and cloves. Pulse, turning the machine quickly on and off, until the peanuts are finely chopped. Remove the spiced chopped peanuts and set aside.

3. Heat the oil in a large nonstick skillet or Dutch oven. Add the pork cubes and cook over medium-high heat, turning often, until browned all over, 5 to 7 minutes. With a slotted spoon, remove the pork to a plate.

4. Add the onion to the skillet, reduce the heat to medium and cook, stirring occasionally, until soft and starting to brown, about 5 minutes. Add the garlic and cook until soft and fragrant, 1 to 2 minutes longer. Return the pork to the pan along with any juices that have collected on the plate.

5. Add the chicken broth, chile purée, chopped spiced peanuts, orange juice concentrate and vinegar. Cover, reduce the heat to medium-low and simmer until the pork is very tender, 45 to 50 minutes. Add the pineapple and peaches and simmer, uncovered, 5 minutes longer.

Green Chile Pork Stew

This hearty stew makes a rib-sticking lunch or dinner on a cold winter day. The mix of greens is packed with vitamins and minerals, but is extremely low in calories. This is a soupy stew with a lot of liquid, so be sure to serve it in deep bowls.

6 SERVINGS   332 CALORIES PER SERVING

> 1 tablespoon olive oil
> 1½ pounds boneless pork loin, trimmed of fat and cut into 1-inch cubes
> 1 large white onion, chopped
> 6 garlic cloves, sliced
> ¾ pound red potatoes, scrubbed and cut into 1-inch pieces
> 1 can (27 ounces) whole roasted peeled green chiles—drained, rinsed and puréed in the blender
> 2 teaspoons dried oregano
> 3 cups unsalted or reduced-sodium chicken broth
> ½ pound fresh kale, rinsed, stems removed and leaves cut into ½-inch-wide strips
> ½ pound fresh mustard greens, thick stems removed and leaves cut into ½-inch-wide strips
> ½ pound fresh spinach, rinsed thoroughly, stems removed and leaves cut into ½-inch-wide strips
> 1 teaspoon salt
> ½ teaspoon freshly ground black pepper

1. Heat the oil in a large Dutch oven. Add the pork cubes and cook over medium-high heat, turning, until browned all over, 6 to 8 minutes. With a slotted spoon, remove the pork to a plate.

2. Add the onion to the Dutch oven, reduce the heat to medium and cook, stirring occasionally, until the onion is beginning to brown, about 5 minutes. Add the garlic and cook, stirring often, 2 minutes longer.

3. Return the pork to the pan along with any juices that have collected on the plate. Add the potatoes, chile purée, oregano and chicken broth. Cover and simmer over medium heat 30 minutes.

4. Add the kale, mustard greens and more chicken broth, if necessary, and cook 10 minutes longer. Add the spinach and cook until the pork and all the greens are tender and the potatoes cooked through, another 10 minutes. Season with the salt and pepper and ladle into serving bowls.

Pork in Salsa Verde

379 Calories per serving

1 teaspoon ground cumin
3 garlic cloves, minced
1 teaspoon salt
2½ pounds boneless pork loin, trimmed of all fat and cut into ¾-inch
   cubes
2 tablespoons olive oil
1 medium onion, chopped
3 fresh jalapeño peppers, stems removed and seeded
3 cans (11 ounces each) tomatillos, drained
1 cup reduced-sodium chicken broth
½ teaspoon dried oregano
Vegetable cooking spray
¼ cup chopped fresh cilantro or parsley

1. In a small bowl, mix the cumin, half the garlic and the salt. In a medium bowl, combine the pork with the cumin mixture and toss well to coat the meat with the seasonings. Cover the bowl with plastic wrap and let stand at room temperature for 2 hours or refrigerate overnight.

2. Heat the olive oil in a large nonstick skillet over medium heat. Add the onion and the remaining garlic and cook until softened, 3 to 4 minutes. Scrape this mixture into a blender or food processor. Add the jalapeño peppers, tomatillos, chicken broth and oregano. Purée until smooth, 1 to 2 minutes.

3. Spray the same large nonstick skillet with vegetable cooking spray and heat over medium-high heat. Add half the pork cubes to the skillet and cook, turning, until browned on all sides, 5 to 7 minutes. With a slotted spoon, remove the meat to a plate and brown the remaining pork.

4. Return all the meat to the skillet. Add the tomatillo purée and simmer until the sauce is thickened, 8 to 10 minutes. Stir in the cilantro and serve.

Rabbit Stew with Vegetables

Rabbit provides another light meat alternative for people counting calories, and if you have never tried it, you'll find it a delicate, mild-flavored meat, much like chicken. In fact, if rabbit is unavailable, you can substitute a 3½-pound fryer, cut into serving pieces. The cooking time will remain the same.

6 SERVINGS   390 CALORIES PER SERVING

> 1 rabbit (3 to 3½ pounds), cut into 8 serving pieces
> 1 teaspoon salt
> ½ teaspoon freshly ground black pepper
> ½ teaspoon ground cinnamon
> ¼ teaspoon ground cloves
> 2 tablespoons olive oil
> 1 medium white onion, chopped
> 4 garlic cloves, minced
> 1 bay leaf
> ½ teaspoon dried thyme
> ½ teaspoon dried oregano
> 5 cups unsalted or reduced-sodium chicken broth
> 3 medium carrots, peeled and cut into ½-inch dice
> ¾ pound small red potatoes, cut into ½-inch dice
> 2 medium zucchini, cut into ½-inch dice
> ½ pound mushrooms, quartered
> 1 tablespoon cornstarch

1. Arrange the rabbit pieces on a platter. Season with the salt, pepper, cinnamon and cloves, cover with plastic wrap and let stand at room temperature 30 minutes.

2. Heat 1 tablespoon of the oil in a large Dutch oven or preferably nonstick skillet. Add the rabbit and cook over medium-high heat, turning, until browned all over, 6 to 8 minutes. Remove to a plate with tongs.

3. Add the remaining 1 tablespoon oil and the onion to the Dutch oven. Cook over medium-high heat, stirring often, until the onion is soft, 3 to 5 minutes. Add the garlic and cook, stirring often, 1 minute longer.

4. Add the bay leaf, thyme, oregano and chicken broth and bring to a boil. Add the rabbit pieces, reduce the heat to medium-low, cover and simmer 30 minutes.

5. Add the carrots and potatoes and simmer 20 minutes. Add the zucchini and mushrooms and cook until the rabbit and all the vegetables are tender, about 10 minutes longer.

6. Stir the cornstarch into 3 tablespoons cold water until blended and smooth. Stir into the stew and bring to a boil, stirring until the sauce is thickened. Reduce the heat and simmer 2 minutes.

Grilled Flank Steak with Black and White Chili Beans

This is a great party dish, an upscale version of barbecued beef and refried beans. While beans are healthy in that they contain no fat or cholesterol, they are high in calories, so portion control is important.

8 SERVINGS   201 CALORIES PER SERVING

> *1½ tablespoons olive oil*
> *2 tablespoons fresh lime juice*
> *2 small garlic cloves, crushed through a press*
> *½ teaspoon dried oregano*
> *1 teaspoon salt*
> *½ teaspoon freshly ground black pepper*
> *Pinch of cayenne pepper*
> *2 pounds flank steak, trimmed of all visible fat*
> *Black and White Chili Beans (recipe follows)*

1. In a small bowl, combine the olive oil, lime juice, garlic, oregano, salt and peppers; blend well. Rub this mixture over both sides of the steak and put on a platter. Cover the meat with plastic wrap and marinate at room temperature 30 minutes.

2. Light a hot fire in a grill or preheat your broiler. Remove the steak from the marinade and pat dry with paper towels. Grill or broil the flank steak about 4 inches from the heat, turning once, 4 to 6 minutes per side for medium-rare, or until cooked to the desired degree of doneness.

3. Transfer the steak to a carving board and let stand 5 minutes before carving on a slant crosswise against the grain into thin slices. Serve with the Black and White Chili Beans on the side.

Black and White Chili Beans

8 Servings   110 Calories per serving

1 medium onion, chopped
1 garlic clove, minced
1 tablespoon olive oil
1 tablespoon chili powder
1 teaspoon ground cumin
½ teaspoon dried oregano
½ teaspoon salt
¼ teaspoon freshly ground black pepper
1 tablespoon tomato paste
1½ cups unsalted or reduced-sodium chicken broth
1 can (16 ounces) black beans, drained and rinsed
1 can (16 ounces) white beans, drained and rinsed
2 tablespoons chopped fresh parsley, for garnish

1. In a large nonstick skillet or Dutch oven, cook the onion and garlic in the olive oil over medium-high heat, stirring occasionally, until pale golden, about 5 minutes. Add the chili powder, cumin, oregano, salt and pepper. Cook, stirring, 1 minute longer.

2. Remove from the heat and add the tomato paste. Then gradually stir in the chicken broth. Return to the heat, bring to a boil, reduce the heat to medium-low and simmer until the sauce is slightly thickened, 10 to 15 minutes. Add the beans and simmer 10 minutes longer. Garnish with parsley before serving.

Lamb and Red Chile Stew Jalisco

Back in Jalisco, where this stew originated, cooks like to make the dish with a dried pepper called the *chile guajillo,* which is tarter and much hotter than the dried ancho peppers most readily available in this country. If you do have access to them, use 3 anchos and 2 guajillos.

There's a lot of complex-flavored sauce here, so serve with warm tortillas or steamed rice. Because the stew is even better reheated the next day, it makes a marvelous dish for entertaining.

5 dried ancho or 4 New Mexican dried red chile peppers
2 cups boiling water
2 medium white onions, chopped
½ cup unsalted or reduced-sodium chicken broth
½ cup orange juice
2 tablespoons red wine vinegar
6 garlic cloves, minced
1½ teaspoons salt
½ teaspoon freshly ground black pepper
½ teaspoon dried oregano
½ teaspoon dried thyme
1 can (28 ounces) Italian-style plum tomatoes, with their juices
2 bay leaves
3 pounds boneless leg of lamb, well trimmed and cut into 2-inch
    chunks
2 limes, cut into wedges, for garnish

Meat

133

1. Preheat the oven to 325° F. Remove the stems from the chiles and tap out the seeds. Place the chiles in a medium heatproof bowl and cover with the boiling water. Let stand until soft, about 30 minutes.

2. In a blender or food processor, combine half the chopped onions, the chicken broth, orange juice, vinegar, 3 of the garlic cloves, salt, pepper, oregano and thyme. Lift out the chiles from their soaking liquid and add them to the blender. Slowly pour in the chile water, discarding the residue at the bottom of the bowl. Purée until smooth. Set this chile sauce aside.

3. Cut the tomatoes in half and place in a large nonaluminum Dutch oven along with their juices. Add the bay leaves and the lamb. Sprinkle on the remaining onion and garlic. Add the chile sauce, cover and bake until the lamb shreds easily with a fork, about 2 hours.

4. With a slotted spoon, transfer the lamb to a side dish. Let the sauce stand for 10 or 15 minutes, then skim off all visible fat from the surface. Remove and discard the bay leaves. Purée the sauce in batches, if necessary, in a blender or food processor. Return to the Dutch oven.

5. Shred the lamb coarsely and add to the pot. Rewarm over medium heat to simmering, or cover and refrigerate overnight before reheating. If necessary, thin the sauce with a little additional orange juice or water. To serve, ladle the meat and sauce into bowls and garnish each portion with a lime wedge.

Mexican Pepper Steak

6 SERVINGS   385 CALORIES PER SERVING

2 tablespoons olive oil
1 medium onion, sliced
3 fresh jalapeño peppers, seeded and cut lengthwise into thin strips, or
  1 can (4 ounces) whole green chiles, seeded and cut into ¼-inch-
  wide strips
1 can (16 ounces) crushed tomatoes
½ teaspoon dried oregano
1 teaspoon salt
½ teaspoon freshly ground black pepper
1½ pounds beef tenderloin, cut into 2 × ½-inch strips
2 tablespoons chopped cilantro or parsley

1. In a large nonstick skillet, heat 1 tablespoon of the oil over medium-high heat. Add the onion and cook until soft, about 3 minutes. Add the jalapeño pepper strips and cook, stirring often, until the onion is beginning to color and the jalapeños are softened, about 3 minutes longer. Add the tomatoes and oregano and simmer until thickened, 12 to 15 minutes. Scrape the mixture into a bowl and season with the salt and pepper. Wipe out the skillet.

2. Heat the remaining 1 tablespoon oil in the skillet over medium-high heat. Add the strips of beef and cook, turning and tossing often, until browned outside but still very rare inside, 2 to 3 minutes. Pour the tomato-onion-jalapeño pepper mixture over the steak, reduce the heat to medium and cook, stirring often, until the dish is heated through and the beef is cooked to the desired degree of doneness, 3 to 5 minutes; tenderloin of beef is best on the rare side. Sprinkle cilantro over the top and serve.

Chapter Six

VEGETABLES, SALADS AND SIDE DISHES

Many of the vegetables eaten in Mexico are those the Spanish brought with them from Europe: cabbage, cucumbers, garlic, lettuce, radishes, peas and beets. Others common in their cooking have their roots in the New World: avocados, beans, tomatoes, both sweet bell peppers and hot chiles, corn, squash, potatoes and those two distinctly Mexican specialties *nopales,* which are the paddle-like leaves of the nopal cactus, and jicama, a crisp root vegetable that is eaten raw. Rice was introduced later through a more circuitous root, but it is used extensively.

These healthful carbohydrates, sometimes mixed with a little cheese, make up a significant proportion of the typical Mexican diet. Many appetizers and snacks, salsas, stews and soups are vegetarian or contain significant quantities of raw or cooked vegetables. Tortilla dishes are liberally garnished with shredded lettuce, onions, radishes and cucumbers.

While refried beans and Spanish rice, popular dishes on their own, are not usually served in combination with tacos and enchiladas in Mexico, they certainly are up North, and I've created the lightest possible version of these favorites. For the beans, a tiny amount of olive oil and flavorful chicken broth takes the place of copious quantities of lard. My Spanish rice is kept lean by omitting the ham or sausage sometimes added and by limiting the olive oil to a single tablespoon.

In this chapter you'll find a mix of refreshing salads, often dressed with lime juice or vinegar, a little oil and chicken broth to add the extra moisture and flavor. Many are a mixture of vegetables colorful and crisp.

Fiesta Slaw, for example, tosses together green cabbage with cucumber, scallions, red and yellow peppers, celery and carrot; Jicama, Orange and Watercress Salad with Citrus Vinaigrette is a more composed melange, refreshing with its juxtaposition of sweet orange and slightly bitter watercress. There are stuffed vegetables, rice dishes and three intriguing ways to prepare that Mexican favorite, corn: a bright relish/salad, an utterly simply but superb Grilled Sweet Corn and a Corn Pudding that will astound you with its lightness. Each individual serving in this chapter adds up to 175 calories or less.

Refried Pinto Beans

Beans are low in fat and have no cholesterol, but they are packed with calories. Cooking them in chicken broth, rather than frying them in lard or oil, keeps the count to a minimum, and lets you enjoy a lighter version of this classic accompaniment to all kinds of tacos and other typical Mexican dishes.

6 SERVINGS   113 CALORIES PER SERVING

1 small white onion, diced
1 tablespoon olive oil
2 garlic cloves, minced
2 cans (16 ounces each) pinto beans, rinsed and drained
1 cup unsalted or reduced-sodium chicken broth
1/4 teaspoon salt
1/4 teaspoon freshly ground black pepper

1. In a large nonstick skillet, cook the onion in the olive oil over medium heat, stirring occasionally, until soft and beginning to color, about 5 minutes. Add the garlic and cook, stirring often, until golden brown, 2 to 3 minutes longer.

2. Add one-third of the beans and 1/4 cup of the chicken broth to the skillet. Coarsely mash the beans with a potato masher or a wooden spoon. Add another third of the beans and another 1/4 cup chicken broth and coarsely mash these beans. Finally, add the remaining beans and another 1/4 cup chicken broth and mash those beans, too.

3. Stir in the remaining 1/4 cup broth and season with the salt and pepper. Bring to a simmer over medium heat and cook, stirring almost constantly with a wooden spoon, until the beans are very thick, 10 to 15 minutes.

— *Green and Yellow Bean Salad with Tomato* —

6 SERVINGS   77 CALORIES PER SERVING

½ pound fresh green beans
½ pound fresh wax beans
Vegetable cooking spray
½ medium white onion, thinly sliced
6 plum tomatoes, sliced into rounds ¼ inch thick
2 tablespoons chopped parsley
¼ cup chicken broth or water
2 tablespoons red wine vinegar
½ teaspoon salt
¼ teaspoon freshly ground black pepper
2 tablespoons olive oil

1. Fill a large saucepan about three-fourths full with lightly salted water and bring to a boil. Add the green beans and wax beans and cook until crisp-tender, 3 to 5 minutes. Drain the beans in a colander and rinse under cold running water; drain well.

2. Coat a nonstick skillet with vegetable cooking spray and cook the onion over medium heat until softened, 3 to 4 minutes. Scrape the onion into a medium bowl, add the cooked beans, tomatoes and parsley and toss.

3. In a small bowl, combine the broth, vinegar, salt and pepper. Whisk in the olive oil and drizzle the dressing over the vegetables. Toss and serve.

Ensalada Mixta

6 SERVINGS   75 CALORIES PER SERVING

2 cups finely shredded romaine or iceberg lettuce
1 cup finely shredded green cabbage
1 cup finely shredded red cabbage
2 medium carrots, peeled and coarsely shredded
1 medium red bell pepper, cut into thin strips
1 medium green bell pepper, cut into thin strips

¼ cup plus 2 tablespoons unsalted or reduced-sodium chicken broth
3 tablespoons cider vinegar
2 tablespoons olive oil
½ teaspoon salt
¼ teaspoon freshly ground black pepper
2 teaspoons sugar

1. In a large bowl, combine the lettuce, the green cabbage, red cabbage, carrots and red and green bell peppers. Toss lightly.

2. In a small bowl, combine the chicken broth, vinegar, olive oil, salt, pepper and sugar. Whisk until blended. Pour the dressing over the salad and toss until coated.

—— *Wilted Spinach with Crushed Red Pepper* ——

Spinach is loaded with iron and high in vitamins A and D. To maximize iron absorption, serve with a meat dish, particularly beef or pork.

4 SERVINGS   59 CALORIES PER SERVING

1 teaspoon olive oil
1 medium red onion, diced
1 garlic clove, minced
1½ pounds fresh spinach, rinsed thoroughly and dried
¼ teaspoon crushed hot red pepper
½ teaspoon salt
¼ teaspoon freshly ground black pepper
1½ tablespoons sherry vinegar or red wine vinegar

1. Heat the olive oil in a large nonstick skillet. Add the onion and cook over medium-high heat until soft, about 3 minutes. Add the garlic and cook until soft and fragrant, about 1 minute longer.

2. Add the spinach, hot pepper, salt and black pepper and toss. Cook, uncovered, tossing occasionally, until the spinach is wilted but still bright green, 3 to 5 minutes. Sprinkle the vinegar over the spinach, toss and serve immediately.

Roasted Beet Salad

4 Servings   88 Calories per serving

1 pound medium beets, with tops
¼ cup finely diced white onion
¼ cup unsalted or reduced-sodium chicken broth
2 tablespoons red wine vinegar
1 tablespoon sugar
½ teaspoon ground cumin
¼ teaspoon salt
¼ teaspoon freshly ground black pepper
1 tablespoon olive oil
1 large bunch of watercress

1. Preheat the oven to 350° F. Trim the beet greens to within 1 inch of the beets. Wrap in a double layer of aluminum foil and roast 45 minutes to 1 hour, or until the beets are tender when tested with the tip of a knife.

2. Cut the stems off the beets and peel off the skin. Cut the beets into ¼-inch slices, then cut the slices into ¼-inch strips. Place in a medium bowl.

3. In a small bowl, combine the onion, chicken broth, vinegar, sugar, cumin, salt and pepper. Whisk until the sugar dissolves, then whisk in the olive oil until blended. Pour the dressing over the beets and toss to coat thoroughly. Cover with plastic wrap and let marinate 1 hour at room temperature, tossing often.

4. Trim any tough stems from the watercress. Arrange the watercress on a platter or divide evenly among 4 salad plates. Spoon the marinated beets onto the watercress and serve at room temperature.

Corn Relish

This "relish" is really a tart cooked salad that is excellent warm, at room temperature or even slightly chilled. It makes a fine accompaniment to grilled chicken and meats.

6 Servings   74 Calories per serving

> 1 tablespoon corn or olive oil
> 1 medium white onion, diced
> 2 cups corn kernels, preferably fresh
> 1 medium red bell pepper, diced
> 1/3 cup diced fresh poblano chile or green bell pepper
> 2 tablespoons chopped cilantro or parsley
> 1 1/2 tablespoons fresh lime juice or white wine vinegar
> 1/2 teaspoon salt

1. Heat the oil in a large nonstick skillet. Add the onion and cook, stirring occasionally, until soft, about 3 minutes. Add the corn and continue to cook until the onion is lightly colored and the corn is just tender, 3 to 5 minutes. Scrape into a medium bowl.

2. Add the red bell pepper, poblano chile, cilantro, lime juice and salt. Toss to mix. Serve at room temperature, or cover and refrigerate for up to 2 days. For best flavor, serve at room temperature.

Chiles Stuffed with Corn and Zucchini

Southof the border, these are called *chiles rellenos,* and they typify the flavors of Mexico. On its own, the filling makes a perfect light accompaniment to grilled fish or chicken.

4 SERVINGS   171 CALORIES PER SERVING

> *8 small fresh Anaheim chiles, about 5 inches long and 1½ inches wide,*
>   *or 4 medium fresh poblano chiles, or 8 large whole canned roasted*
>   *green chiles, rinsed and patted dry*
> *2 teaspoons corn or olive oil*
> *1 medium white onion, chopped*
> *¾ cup corn kernels—fresh, canned or thawed frozen*
> *1 large zucchini (about 8 ounces), cut into ⅜-inch dice*
> *1 tablespoon chopped cilantro or parsley*
> *1 teaspoon chopped fresh oregano or marjoram or ½ teaspoon dried*
> *½ teaspoon salt*
> *¼ teaspoon freshly ground black pepper*
> *Vegetable cooking spray*
> *½ recipe Mexican Tomato Sauce (p. 61), Chipotle Tomato Sauce (p.*
>   *59) or 1½ cups of your favorite prepared brand*
> *½ cup shredded reduced-fat Muenster or Monterey Jack cheese*

1. If you are using fresh chiles, blacken them directly over a gas flame or broil them as close to the heat as possible, turning, until charred all over, about 10 minutes. Place the blackened peppers in a brown paper bag and let steam 10 to 15 minutes. Peel the skin from the peppers and rinse them under cold running water. With the tip of a small, sharp knife, make a slit running from the stem end down to the tip of each chile. Pull out the seeds from inside the chile, being careful not to tear the chile. If you are using canned chiles, you will only need to spread them open to stuff them.

2. Heat the oil in a large nonstick skillet. Add the onion and cook until soft, about 3 minutes. Add the corn and zucchini and cook over medium heat, stirring occasionally, until the squash is just tender, 5 to 7 minutes. Add the cilantro and oregano and season with the salt and pepper. Mix well and scrape into a medium bowl. Let cool slightly.

3. If using the smaller Anaheim chiles, fill with about 2 tablespoons of the filling. For the fresh poblanos, use about ¼ cup for each. Do not fill the chiles so much that you can't fold them closed. For the canned chiles, you will need about 1½ to 2 tablespoons of filling for each. Press the opening of each chile closed with your fingers.

4. Preheat the oven to 350° F. Coat an 8-inch square baking dish with vegetable cooking spray and arrange the chiles in it side by side. Pour the tomato sauce over the chiles to coat evenly. Sprinkle the cheese on top. Bake 15 to 20 minutes, until the cheese is melted and the chiles are warmed through.

Grilled Sweet Corn

No butter is needed with this savory way of preparing corn. The smokiness of the grill and tartness of the lime blend beautifully with the sweetness of fresh corn.

6 SERVINGS   81 CALORIES PER SERVING

> *6 ears of fresh corn in the husk*
> *1 lime, cut into 6 wedges*
> *Salt and ground ancho chile powder or hot paprika (optional)*

1. Soak the unhusked corn in water 1 hour. Meanwhile, light a hot fire in a grill and set the rack 4 inches from the coals. When the fire is ready, shake any excess water from the ears of corn and place them directly on the grill. Roast, turning often, until the outer husks are charred, about 15 to 20 minutes. Remove the ears from the heat and let stand until cool enough to handle, 10 to 15 minutes.

2. Strip the husks from the ears and remove the cornsilk. Return the corn to the grill and roast the ears, turning often, until lightly browned, 3 to 4 minutes. Serve the corn with wedges of lime and a sprinkling of salt and ground ancho chile powder.

Corn Pudding

This savory baked pudding is a perfect side dish with roasted or grilled meats. Substituting egg whites for some of the whole eggs reduces the cholesterol—and the calories—without diminishing the satisfaction.

6 Servings   175 Calories per serving

2 tablespoons unsalted butter
1 medium onion, chopped
1 garlic clove, minced
Kernels cut from 6 large ears of corn, or 2 packages (10 ounces each)
   frozen corn, thawed
1 whole egg
2 egg whites
1 can (5 ounces) evaporated milk
1 teaspoon dried marjoram or oregano
1 teaspoon salt
½ teaspoon freshly ground black pepper
Vegetable cooking spray

1. Preheat the oven to 350° F. Melt the butter in a large nonstick skillet. Add the onion and garlic and cook over medium heat, stirring occasionally, until softened, 3 to 5 minutes. Add the corn and cook, stirring often, until the onion is golden and the corn is just tender, about 3 minutes longer. Remove from the heat.

2. In a large bowl, beat the whole egg and egg whites until blended. Whisk in the evaporated milk and season with the marjoram, salt and pepper. Scrape the onion and corn from the skillet into the bowl and mix well.

3. Coat an 8-inch square baking dish with vegetable cooking spray. Pour in the corn mixture and bake 45 to 50 minutes, until set and golden on top. Serve piping hot.

Savory Cornmeal Muffins

MAKES 24 SMALL MUFFINS   52 CALORIES PER MUFFIN

Vegetable cooking spray
³/₄ cup unbleached all-purpose flour
³/₄ cup yellow cornmeal
2 tablespoons sugar
1¹/₂ teaspoons baking powder
³/₄ teaspoon salt
1 large egg
¹/₃ cup low-fat buttermilk
2 tablespoons corn or peanut oil
¹/₄ cup finely chopped onion
1 large garlic clove, minced
³/₄ teaspoon dried oregano
1 jar (4 ounces) diced roasted red peppers, drained
1 can (4 ounces) diced green chiles, drained

1. Preheat the oven to 350° F. Coat 2 miniature muffin tins lightly with vegetable cooking spray.

2. In a large bowl, combine the flour, cornmeal, sugar, baking powder and salt. Whisk gently to mix. Make a well in the center of the dry ingredients.

3. In a medium bowl, beat the egg until blended. Whisk in the buttermilk and oil until well blended. Mix in the onion, garlic, oregano, roasted peppers and green chiles. Pour this mixture into the well in the center of the dry ingredients and stir until blended and evenly moistened; do not overmix.

4. With a tablespoon, fill each muffin cup even with the top. Bake the muffins until they are fully risen and cooked through, 15 to 20 minutes. Let the pans cool on wire racks 15 minutes before unmolding the muffins.

Jicama, Orange and Watercress Salad with Citrus Vinaigrette

Here's an exceptionally light salad that's particularly refreshing because of the sweet-tart contrast between the orange and the vinaigrette dressing. There is the pleasing crunch of jicama as well.

4 SERVINGS   136 CALORIES PER SERVING

> *2 large bunches of watercress*
> *1 pound jicama*
> *2 medium navel oranges*
> *4 thin slices of red onion, separated into rings*
> *¼ cup Citrus Vinaigrette (recipe follows)*

1. Remove any tough stems from the watercress and discard. Peel the tough brown skin from the jicama with a paring knife or swivel-bladed vegetable peeler. With a large knife, cut the jicama into ¼-inch slices, then cut the slices into thin sticks.

2. With a small sharp knife, peel the outer orange skin and white pith from the oranges. Remove the individual segments by holding a peeled orange in one hand over a bowl to catch the juices and cutting down both sides of each membrane in a V-shape. Squeeze the membranes over the bowl to extract as much juice as possible.

3. Mound the watercress on 4 salad plates. Scatter the jicama around the watercress. Divide the orange segments among the salads and garnish with the red onion rings. Drizzle 2 tablespoons of the Citrus Vinaigrette over each salad.

Citrus Vinaigrette

Orange, lemon and lime juice acts as a substitute for oil in this light dressing, while adding an agreeably tart flavor. Refrigerated in a covered jar, the vinaigrette will keep well for up to 3 days.

MAKES ABOUT 1 CUP   21 CALORIES PER TABLESPOON

1 large orange
1 large lime
1 lemon
2 tablespoons frozen orange juice concentrate
1 tablespoon white wine vinegar
3 tablespoons olive oil
2 large shallots, minced
2 tablespoons chopped parsley
1/2 teaspoon salt
1/4 teaspoon freshly ground black pepper

1. Grate the zest of the orange into a small bowl. Cut the orange in half and squeeze the juice into the bowl. Do the same with the lime and the lemon.

2. Whisk in the orange juice concentrate, vinegar and olive oil. Add the shallots, parsley, salt and pepper and stir to dissolve the salt. Let stand 30 minutes at room temperature before using.

Salad of Romaine, Tomato and Avocado with Avocado Dressing

6 SERVINGS   114 CALORIES PER SERVING

1 large head of romaine lettuce
2 medium ripe tomatoes, cored and cut into 18 wedges
1 medium avocado, peeled and cut into 12 slices
6 scallions, thinly sliced
Salt and freshly ground black pepper
1 lime, cut into 6 wedges
Avocado Dressing (recipe follows)

1. Separate the romaine leaves; rinse and dry. Divide the leaves among 6 salad bowls. Scatter the tomato, avocado and scallions evenly on top of the romaine and season with salt to taste. Squeeze the juice of one wedge of lime over each salad.

2. Drizzle 1/4 cup of Avocado Dressing over each salad.

Avocado Dressing

MAKES ABOUT 1½ CUPS   44 CALORIES PER ¼ CUP SERVING

½ medium avocado
½ cup plain nonfat yogurt
¾ cup skim milk
1 tablespoon cider vinegar
¼ cup chopped onion
2 tablespoons chopped fresh cilantro
½ teaspoon salt
¼ teaspoon white pepper (optional)

Place all the ingredients in a blender or food processor and purée for 1 to 2 minutes. Taste and adjust seasonings.

Nopalitos

Nopalitos are the paddle-shaped "leaves" of the nopal cactus. In Mexico they are reputed to be very good for your health.

6 SERVINGS   74 CALORIES PER SERVING

1 can (28 ounces) cactus paddles, rinsed and drained (see Note)
1 large ripe tomato, cut into ½-inch dice
1 medium red onion, thinly sliced
3 to 4 fresh jalapeño or other hot green chile peppers, seeded and cut
    lengthwise into thin strips
¼ cup chopped cilantro or parsley
¼ cup fresh lime juice
2 tablespoons extra virgin olive oil
½ teaspoon freshly ground black pepper
¼ teaspoon salt

In a large bowl, combine the cactus paddles, tomato, red onion, jalapeño peppers, cilantro, lime juice, olive oil, pepper and salt. Toss to mix well. Cover and refrigerate if not serving within 1 hour.

NOTE *The canned cactus for this recipe is sold under different descriptions—as "cactus paddles," "nopalitos" and "tender cactus in light brine." They are available in Mexican markets and in the Latin American food section of many supermarkets.*

Fiesta Slaw

It's the tricolored mix of peppers here that gives this salad its festive appearance, but if yellow bell peppers are not available in your market, use 2 red bell peppers or substitute 1 large green pepper.

6 SERVINGS   69 CALORIES PER SERVING

> *1 pound green cabbage*
> *1 medium cucumber, peeled*
> *5 scallions, thinly sliced*
> *1 medium red bell pepper, cut into thin strips*
> *1 medium yellow bell pepper, cut into thin strips*
> *2 celery ribs, thinly sliced*
> *1 large carrot, peeled and cut into thin strips 2 inches long*
> *3 tablespoons fresh lime juice*
> *2 tablespoons white wine vinegar*
> *½ to 1 teaspoon hot pepper sauce*
> *3 tablespoons sugar*
> *1 teaspoon salt*

1. Shred the cabbage in a food processor or on the slicing blade of a hand grater. Cut the cucumber in half, scoop out the seeds with a spoon and thinly slice. In a large serving bowl, combine the shredded cabbage, sliced cucumber, scallions, red and yellow bell peppers, celery and carrot. Toss lightly to mix.

2. In a small bowl, combine the lime juice, vinegar, hot sauce, sugar, salt and 2 tablespoons water. Stir until the sugar dissolves.

3. Pour the dressing over the vegetables and toss well. Let stand at room temperature 30 minutes, tossing often, before serving. For maximum color and flavor serve within 3 hours.

– *Salad of Roasted Peppers, Tomatoes and Cheese* –

A wonderful light first course in summer or winter, this salad combines some of Mexico's finest flavors. South of the border, the cheese in the salad would be *queso fresco,* a freshly made, crumbly cheese quite unlike anything readily available north of the Rio Grande.

4 SERVINGS   147 CALORIES PER SERVING

> 2 medium red bell peppers or 1 jar (7 ounces) roasted red peppers,
>   drained
> 1 can (4 ounces) whole roasted green chiles, drained and cut into thin
>   strips
> 2 large tomatoes, cut into ¼-inch slices
> 4 ounces unsalted reduced-fat fresh mozzarella cheese or reduced-fat
>   goat cheese, cut into ¼-inch slices, or feta cheese, crumbled
> ½ medium red onion, thinly sliced
> 1 tablespoon plus 1 teaspoon extra virgin olive oil
> 1 tablespoon fresh lime juice
> ½ teaspoon salt
> ¼ teaspoon freshly ground black pepper

1. If using fresh bell peppers, blacken the skins directly over a gas flame or broil them as close to the heat as possible, turning, until charred all over, about 10 minutes. Put the blackened peppers in a paper bag and let cool. Peel off the charred skin and rinse the peppers under cold running water. Remove the stems and seeds from the peppers and cut into strips. If using roasted peppers from a jar, simply cut them into strips.

2. On each of 4 salad plates, arrange one-fourth of the tomato slices, cheese and red onion. Scatter the roasted pepper and green chile strips over the salads, dividing them evenly.

3. In a small bowl, whisk together the olive oil, lime juice, salt, pepper and 2 tablespoons water. Spoon about 1 tablespoon of dressing evenly over each salad and serve.

Mexican Potato Salad

Other low-calorie vegetables, such as carrots and celery, help stretch the portions here. A vinaigrette dressing mixed with flavorful broth and a minimum of oil is used in place of mayonnaise to keep this salad light.

6 SERVINGS   154 CALORIES PER SERVING

> *1½ pounds medium boiling potatoes*
> *2 medium carrots, peeled and cut into ½-inch dice*
> *¼ cup unsalted or reduced-sodium chicken broth*
> *2 tablespoons white wine vinegar*
> *2 tablespoons juice from pickled jalapeño peppers*
> *2 tablespoons extra virgin olive oil*
> *2 celery ribs, thinly sliced*
> *½ cup chopped white onion*
> *⅓ cup thinly sliced scallion greens*
> *½ cup frozen peas, thawed*
> *3 tablespoons minced pickled jalapeño peppers*
> *¾ teaspoon salt*
> *½ teaspoon freshly ground black pepper*
> *Chopped cilantro or parsley, for garnish*

1. In a large saucepan of boiling water, cook the potatoes until tender to the center, 15 to 20 minutes. Drain and let stand until cool enough to handle; then peel off the skins and cut the potatoes into 1-inch cubes.

2. Meanwhile, in a small saucepan of boiling water, cook the carrots until just tender, about 5 minutes. Drain well.

3. In a medium bowl, toss the warm potatoes and the carrots with the chicken broth, vinegar, pickled jalapeño juice and olive oil. Add the celery, onion, scallion greens, peas and pickled jalapeño peppers. Season with the salt and pepper and toss to mix well. Garnish with chopped cilantro and serve at room temperature or slightly chilled.

Grilled Vegetables

Grilling is a popular form of cooking all over Mexico. While grilled corn, onions and scallions are most typical, the technique works well for any variety of vegetables.

Healthful, sophisticated in taste and at less than 150 calories a portion, these smoky vegetables are almost impossible to resist, and they go well with any number of grilled or simply cooked meats, fish and poultry. If you can afford the calories, a dab of Pumpkin Seed Sauce adds a touch of authenticity and piquant taste.

4 SERVINGS   139 CALORIES PER SERVING

> *1 medium red bell pepper*
> *1 medium zucchini*
> *2 small yellow squash*
> *2 small, narrow Asian eggplant or 1 small regular eggplant*
> *8 large spears of asparagus*
> *12 scallions*
> *3 tablespoons extra virgin olive oil*
> *1½ teaspoons salt*
> *½ teaspoon freshly ground black pepper*
> *Lime wedges or Pumpkin Seed Sauce (recipe follows), as*
> *   accompaniment*

1. Place the red pepper upright on a cutting board and, starting at the top next to the stem, cut straight down to the cutting board on one side. Repeat with the other three sides, then pull the seedless slices away from the stem.

2. Cut the zucchini crosswise on a diagonal into ¼-inch slices. Cut the yellow squash lengthwise in half. If using Asian eggplant, halve it lengthwise; if using a regular eggplant, cut it crosswise into ½-inch rounds. Trim any tough or woody ends from the asparagus spears. Trim off the roots and any ragged tops from the scallions.

3. Spread the prepared vegetables on a baking sheet, brush them lightly with the olive oil and season them with the salt and pepper.

4. Light a hot fire in a grill. Place the vegetables on the grill rack set about 4 inches from the heat and cook, turning, until they are just tender and lightly browned all over. The times will vary for the different vegetables: about 1 to 2 minutes for the scallions, 2 to 3 minutes for the asparagus, 3 to 5 minutes for the peppers, zucchini and yellow squash, and 4 to 6 minutes for the eggplant. Garnish with lime wedges or pass a bowl of the Pumpkin Seed Sauce on the side.

Pumpkin Seed Sauce

Raw shelled pumpkin seeds are available in many supermarkets, at health food stores and, of course, in Mexican food shops, where they are called *pepitas*.

Makes 2½ cups   18 Calories per tablespoon

> 1 small head of garlic
> 3 tablespoons olive oil
> ¾ teaspoon salt
> Pinch of freshly ground black pepper
> 1 cup (about 4 ounces) raw shelled pumpkin seeds (pepitas)
> 1 can (11 ounces) tomatillos, drained and rinsed
> 1 can (4 ounces) whole roasted green chiles, drained and rinsed
> 3 pickled jalapeño peppers
> 2 tablespoons juice from pickled jalapeño peppers
> ¼ cup chopped cilantro or parsley

1. Preheat the oven to 375° F. Remove any loose papery skin from the outside of the head of garlic and cut crosswise in half. Rub the cut surfaces with a few drops of the olive oil and season with a pinch of the salt and pepper. Wrap the garlic in aluminum foil and bake 40 to 45 minutes, until the garlic is soft and golden. Unwrap and let stand until cool enough to handle. Then squeeze the garlic cloves from their skins; they will pop out easily.

2. Meanwhile, in a large nonstick skillet, toast the pumpkin seeds over medium heat, shaking the pan frequently, until the seeds have puffed and turned brighter green, about 3 minutes; do not brown. (The seeds have a tendency to pop, so keep your head back and be careful.) Transfer to a plate or small bowl and let cool.

3. Place the toasted pumpkin seeds in a food processor and pulse until the seeds are finely chopped. Add the roasted garlic, tomatillos, green chiles, pickled jalapeño peppers and their juice, the cilantro and the remaining salt. Pulse until well mixed.

4. With the machine on, gradually add the remaining olive oil, 1 tablespoon at a time. Pulse a few more times. If the sauce seems too thick, blend in a few tablespoons of water. Scrape the sauce into a bowl. If not using immediately, place a piece of plastic wrap directly on top of the sauce, smooth to cover the surface completely and refrigerate.

Stuffed Zucchini Mexicali

Vegetables are the key to light, lower-calorie eating. Here zucchini are stuffed with a tasty mixture of zucchini, corn and chiles, with just a topping of bread crumbs and cheese for a boost of flavor.

6 Servings   59 Calories per serving

> 6 medium-small zucchini, about 6 inches long
> Vegetable cooking spray
> 1 medium onion, minced
> 1 garlic clove, minced
> ½ cup fresh or thawed frozen corn kernels
> 1 can (4 ounces) diced green chiles
> ½ teaspoon dried oregano
> ½ teaspoon salt
> ¼ teaspoon freshly ground black pepper
> 2 tablespoons dried bread crumbs
> 2 tablespoons chopped cilantro or parsley
> 3 tablespoons grated Parmesan cheese
> 1 lime, cut into 6 wedges

1. Preheat the oven to 400° F. Trim off the ends of the zucchini. Cutting lengthwise, slice the top third off each zucchini, mince and reserve. In a large saucepan, bring 8 cups of salted water to a boil. Add the 6 trimmed zucchini and boil 3 minutes, or until slightly softened. Carefully remove the zucchini with tongs and drain on paper towels. Let stand until cool enough to handle. With a teaspoon, scoop out and discard the inside of the zucchini, leaving a ¼- to ½-inch shell.

2. Coat a large nonstick skillet with vegetable cooking spray. Add the onion and garlic and cook over medium-high heat until softened and lightly golden, about 5 minutes. Add the minced zucchini and cook, stirring often, until tender, 3 to 5 minutes. Add the corn, green chiles, oregano, salt and pepper. Cook 3 minutes longer. Remove from the heat.

3. In a medium bowl, combine the zucchini and corn mixture with the bread crumbs, cilantro and Parmesan cheese. Toss to mix. Dry the insides of the zucchini shells with paper towels and spoon the filling into the shells.

4. Spray a 9 × 13-inch baking dish with the cooking spray and place the stuffed zucchini in the dish. Bake until the zucchini are heated through and lightly golden on top, 12 to 15 minutes. Garnish each serving with a lime wedge.

Brown Rice and Black Bean Salad with Artichokes and Red Onion

8 Servings   149 Calories per serving

1 can (16 ounces) black beans, rinsed and drained
2 cups cooked brown rice
1 package (9 ounces) frozen artichoke hearts, thawed, or 1 can (14 ounces) artichoke hearts, rinsed, drained and quartered
1 jar (4 ounces) diced roasted red peppers, rinsed and drained
1 can (4 ounces) diced roasted green chiles, rinsed and drained
1 medium red onion, finely diced
¼ cup chopped cilantro or parsley
2 tablespoons olive oil
2 tablespoons cider vinegar
¼ cup unsalted or reduced-sodium chicken broth
1 teaspoon salt
½ teaspoon freshly ground black pepper

1. In a large serving bowl, combine the beans, rice, artichoke hearts, roasted red peppers, green chiles, onion and cilantro. Toss lightly.

2. In a small bowl, whisk together oil, vinegar, broth, salt and pepper. Pour over the salad and toss once again. Let the salad stand at room temperature 30 minutes. Taste and adjust seasonings. Toss once more before serving.

Rice Casserole with Green Chiles, Mushrooms and Corn

10 SERVINGS   156 CALORIES PER SERVING

1 medium white onion, chopped
1 tablespoon olive oil
1 garlic clove, minced
Kernels from 3 ears of corn or 1 package (10 ounces) frozen corn,
  thawed
¾ pound fresh mushrooms, sliced
2 cans (4 ounces each) diced roasted green chiles, drained
½ teaspoon salt
¼ teaspoon freshly ground black pepper
3 tablespoons chopped cilantro or parsley
3 cups cooked white rice
Vegetable cooking spray
1 cup coarsely grated reduced-fat mozzarella cheese

1. Preheat the oven to 325° F. In a large nonstick skillet, cook the onion in 1½ teaspoons oil over medium-high heat until soft, 3 to 5 minutes. Add the garlic and corn and cook until the garlic is soft and the corn is just tender, 3 to 4 minutes longer. Scrape the mixture into a large bowl.

2. In the same nonstick skillet, cook the mushrooms in the remaining 1½ teaspoons oil over medium-high heat until golden, about 5 minutes. Add the mushrooms to the corn.

3. Add the green chiles, salt, pepper, cilantro and the cooked white rice. Toss to mix thoroughly.

4. Coat a 9 × 13-inch baking dish with vegetable cooking spray. Spoon the rice and vegetables into the dish and spread evenly. Sprinkle the cheese over the top. Bake until the cheese is melted and the rice is heated through, about 20 minutes.

Spanish Rice

8 SERVINGS   150 CALORIES PER SERVING

Vegetable cooking spray
1½ cups long-grain white rice
1 medium white onion, chopped
1 teaspoon finely chopped garlic
1 can (16 ounces) plum tomatoes, puréed with their juice
1¾ cups unsalted or reduced-sodium chicken broth
¼ teaspoon dried oregano
¼ teaspoon salt
¼ teaspoon freshly ground black pepper

1. Coat a medium nonstick skillet with vegetable cooking spray and cook the rice over medium-high heat until it takes on a matte white look and starts to turn golden, 8 to 10 minutes. Scrape the rice into a medium saucepan and set aside.

2. Wipe out the skillet and coat again with the cooking spray. Cook the onion over medium heat until softened, about 3 minutes. Add the garlic and cook until soft and fragrant, about 2 minutes longer.

3. Add the onion and garlic to the rice, along with the puréed tomatoes, chicken broth, oregano, salt and pepper. Bring to a boil over medium heat. Cover and reduce the heat to a simmer. Cook 12 minutes, turn off the heat and let the rice steam itself 10 minutes longer.

Chapter Seven

DESSERTS
AND
BEVERAGES

Custards and fruit are probably the two most common types of Mexican desserts, the former borrowed from the Spanish and the latter a natural with the wealth of vibrantly flavored ripe fruits available in the tropical country. Vanilla and cinnamon, both of which are produced in Mexico, are favorite flavors.

Fruit desserts are easy to enjoy no matter what your calorie limits, and they are nutritious. I've offered several here, some dressed up with Mexico's indigenous liquors—Banana-Strawberry Parfait, laced with tequila, and Tropical Fruit Acapulco, which combines fresh pineapple and banana with just a tablespoon of aged rum for a luscious flavor that is softened by a low-fat yogurt topping. Pink grapefruit and orange lend their tang to *granitas,* coarse-grained ices that are incredibly refreshing, exceptionally low in calories and flavored in an almost infinite variety of ways.

The custards and puddings, while satisfactorily sweet, use the minimum amount of sugar, skim milk and egg whites where possible instead of whole eggs to yield all the delight of the originals with a fraction of the fat and calories.

I've even included one recipe for a typical fried dough dessert, not the usual sort of thing to find in a cookbook devoted to eating light. These simple pastries, dusted with cinnamon sugar, are eaten as a dessert or snack, much as we might eat a doughnut, with a cup of coffee or hot chocolate almost any hour of the day. I wouldn't have dared include this recipe for Sopaipillas until I came up with a version that absorbs so little oil in the frying that the calorie count is well below the limit of 250 set for this chapter.

Because of the heat and altitude of their country, Mexicans consume many beverages, from fresh fruit juices squeezed in stalls on the street to highly sweetened carbonated beverages. I've incorporated recipes for a number of these lighter drinks here, from fruit coolers to spiced coffee. They offer a refreshing way to end a festive Mexican meal.

Natillas

This vanilla-flavored milk dessert is a Mexican favorite. I've lightened it by incorporating beaten egg white into the custard. While there is less of a problem with salmonella in raw egg whites than in the yolks, because of recent concern about the bacteria, be sure to use due caution. Use only fresh, refrigerated, uncracked eggs. Do not serve raw eggs to the very young, very old or the physically infirm.

6 SERVINGS   133 CALORIES PER SERVING

> 2¼ cups skim milk
> ⅓ cup plus 2 tablespoons sugar
> Pinch of salt
> 3 tablespoons plus 1 teaspoon cornstarch
> ½ teaspoon ground cinnamon
> ½ teaspoon freshly grated nutmeg
> 1 whole large egg, separated
> 3 large egg whites
> 1 teaspoon vanilla extract

1. In a medium saucepan, scald 2 cups of the milk, then remove the pan from the heat. In a medium bowl, combine the ⅓ cup sugar, the salt, cornstarch, cinnamon, nutmeg, the remaining ¼ cup milk and the egg yolk. Whisk until well blended and smooth.

2. Add the egg mixture to the hot milk all at once, whisking briskly, and return the pot to high heat. Cook the custard, whisking, until it boils and thickens. Remove from the heat.

3. In a clean dry bowl, beat the 4 egg whites until foamy. Add the remaining 2 tablespoons sugar and beat until the whites hold stiff shiny peaks. Fold the beaten egg whites and the vanilla into the warm custard gently with a rubber spatula.

4. Transfer the natillas to a large serving bowl or divide it evenly among 6 custard cups. Sprinkle additional ground cinnamon over the top and refrigerate until chilled, at least 2 hours, before serving.

Coconut Pudding

Unsweetened coconut is available at health food stores and in many ethnic markets. If you cannot find it, use sweetened coconut and reduce the sugar to 2 tablespoons.

6 SERVINGS   196 CALORIES PER SERVING

2½ cups low-fat (2%) milk
1 cup unsweetened shredded coconut
⅓ cup sugar
3 tablespoons cornstarch
Pinch of salt
1 whole large egg plus 1 egg white, lightly beaten
1 teaspoon vanilla extract

1. In a medium saucepan, warm the milk over medium heat until bubbles appear around the edges, 3 to 5 minutes. (Watch carefully, because if the milk boils it may bubble over the top of the pan.) Add the shredded coconut and half the sugar. Remove the pan from the heat and let the coconut steep in the milk 20 minutes. Transfer the coconut mixture to a blender and purée until smooth.

2. In a medium saucepan, combine the remaining sugar with the cornstarch and salt. Gradually whisk in the coconut purée until well blended, then beat in the beaten egg and egg white. Bring to a boil over medium heat, whisking constantly. Reduce the heat to medium-low and continue to cook, whisking, 2 minutes. Remove from the heat and stir in the vanilla.

3. Let the pudding cool slightly for 10 minutes and serve warm, which is traditional in Mexico. Or spoon into 6 dessert dishes or a serving bowl, cover and refrigerate until chilled before serving.

Rice Pudding

Mexico is a large producer of vanilla, and it is one of that country's favorite dessert flavorings. While the amount called for below may sound extravagant, it produces a mellow, rich-tasting dessert.

8 SERVINGS   212 CALORIES PER SERVING

> *4½ cups low-fat (2%) milk*
> *⅓ cup sugar*
> *Pinch of salt*
> *1¼ cups long-grain white rice*
> *1 tablespoon vanilla extract*
> *¼ teaspoon ground cinnamon*

1. In a medium saucepan, combine 4 cups of the milk with the sugar and salt. Bring barely to a simmer over medium heat, stirring to dissolve the sugar. Remove the pan from the heat.

2. Rinse the rice thoroughly in a fine sieve under cold running water; drain well. Add the rice to the milk and return the pan to medium heat. Bring to a boil, reduce the heat to low, cover and cook, without stirring, until the rice is tender and most of the liquid has been absorbed, about 15 minutes. Do not overcook.

3. Add the remaining ½ cup milk, the vanilla and cinnamon. Raise the heat to medium and cook, stirring constantly, until the pudding begins to thicken, 3 to 5 minutes. Remove the pan from the heat, let cool slightly and serve tepid, or transfer the rice pudding to a serving bowl or individual dessert dishes, cover and refrigerate until slightly chilled.

Dried Fruit Compote

These days there is a wealth of dried fruit available at the health food store and at the grocery. The choices range from currants, dark raisins, golden raisins, apricots and figs to dried blueberries, cranberries and cherries. The larger fruits, such as apricots and figs, are more manageable cut into halves or quarters.

8 SERVINGS   213 CALORIES PER SERVING

> *3 cups dry white wine*
> *1 cup sugar*
> *3 cinnamon sticks*
> *Zest and juice of 1 lemon*
> *Zest and juice of 1 small orange*
> *1½ cups mixed dried fruits, such as apricots, cherries and currants or*
>   *raisins*
> *Fresh mint leaves, for garnish*

1. In a medium nonaluminum saucepan, combine the wine, sugar, cinnamon sticks, lemon zest and juice and the orange zest and juice. Bring to a boil over medium heat, stirring to dissolve the sugar. Boil the syrup 5 minutes.

2. Place the dried fruit in a large heatproof bowl. Pour the syrup over the fruit and let stand at room temperature for 3 hours, then cover and refrigerate until chilled, about 2 hours. Serve the fruit in dessert bowls, with a little of the syrup poured over them. Garnish with fresh mint leaves, if available.

Tropical Fruit Acapulco

After the large Mexican midday multicourse meal, or *comida,* fresh fruit is the most common dessert. Mangoes are served sliced or whole on a plate with a long two-pronged mango fork and knife. Pineapple, papaya and melon are offered simply, with a squeeze of lime. Here is a dressed-up presentation, using our most common tropical fruits—pineapple and banana.

6 SERVINGS   112 CALORIES PER SERVING

> *2 cups diced fresh pineapple*
> *2 tablespoons sugar*
> *1 tablespoon rum, preferably anejo*
> *1 medium banana, thinly sliced*
> *1½ cups low-fat vanilla yogurt*

1. In a medium bowl, toss the pineapple with the sugar and rum. Let macerate, tossing occasionally, 30 minutes. Drain the pineapple, reserving the juices.

2. Return the pineapple to the bowl and toss with the banana slices. In a small bowl, blend the reserved juices with the yogurt.

3. To serve, divide the fruit among 6 dessert bowls. Top with the flavored yogurt. Serve at once.

Vanilla Flan

1⅓ cups sugar
2 whole large eggs, separated
4 egg whites
2⅓ cups skim milk, at room temperature
Pinch of salt
1 tablespoon vanilla extract

1. Prepare a caramel by combining 1 cup of the sugar and ½ cup water in a small saucepan. Stir to dissolve the sugar and bring to a boil over high heat. Cover the pan and boil 10 minutes. Remove the cover and continue to boil until the syrup is light golden brown. Do not stir. Immediately remove from the heat; the caramel will continue to darken. As soon as the bubbling stops, drizzle the hot liquid caramel over the bottom of an 8- or 9-inch round cake pan. Immediately tilt the pan to coat as much of the bottom and sides as you can before the caramel cools and hardens. Don't worry if it's not perfect; it will melt again during cooking.

2. Preheat the oven to 350° F. Place the egg yolks in a medium bowl. Pour all 6 egg whites through a strainer into the bowl to remove any "lumps." Whisk to blend the yolks and whites. Beat in the remaining ⅓ cup sugar, skim milk, salt and vanilla until blended. Pour the custard into the caramel-lined cake pan and set the dish in a roasting pan. Set in the oven and fill the pan with boiling water to reach halfway up the side of the cake pan.

3. Bake 50 to 60 minutes, or until the custard is just set. To test, insert the tip of a small knife into the center. If the blade comes out clean, the custard is done. Carefully remove the pan from the oven. Set the cake pan on a wire rack to cool, then cover with plastic wrap and refrigerate overnight before serving.

4. When you are ready to serve the flan, run a small knife around the rim of the pan to loosen the custard. Invert a serving platter over the pan, turn over and give the cake pan a shake to unmold.

Variation

Espresso Flan: Use a good, strong instant coffee—regular or espresso. Scald 1 cup of the milk in a small saucepan and stir in 4 tablespoons of the instant coffee. Mix this with the remaining 1⅓ cups of milk and proceed with the recipe.

Banana-Strawberry Parfait

6 SERVINGS   78 CALORIES PER SERVING

> *3 ripe bananas*
> *1 tablespoon packed brown sugar*
> *2 teaspoons fresh lime juice*
> *1 tablespoon gold tequila (optional)*
> *¼ teaspoon ground cinnamon*
> *Pinch of ground cloves*
> *1 pint fresh strawberries, halved*

1. In a food processor or blender, combine the bananas, brown sugar, lime juice, tequila, cinnamon and cloves. Purée until smooth.

2. In 6 parfait glasses or glass dessert dishes, layer the berries with the banana purée. Cover and refrigerate until slightly chilled before serving.

Pineapple Gratin

6 SERVINGS   170 CALORIES PER SERVING

⅓ cup chopped pecans
1 medium ripe pineapple
½ cup milk
¼ cup half-and-half
⅓ cup light brown sugar
¼ cup low-calorie orange marmalade
Zest of 1 small orange

1. Preheat the oven to 325° F. Spread out the pecans in a small baking dish and toast in the oven 5 to 7 minutes, or until lightly browned and fragrant. Remove the toasted pecans to a plate. Raise the oven temperature to 375° F.

2. Cut down the length of the pineapple with a large sharp stainless steel knife to remove the skin and "eyes." Cut off the top and bottom of the fruit and quarter the fruit lengthwise. Cut out the core from each large wedge, then cut the pineapple into ½-inch slices. Arrange the pineapple slices in a 9 × 13-inch baking dish.

3. In a medium bowl, combine the milk, half-and-half, brown sugar, marmalade and orange zest. Whisk to blend well. Pour the mixture over the pineapple. Sprinkle the toasted pecans on top.

4. Bake the gratin 40 to 50 minutes, or until the fruit is soft and the top of the dessert is golden brown. Remove to a wire rack and let cool to room temperature before serving.

Pink Grapefruit Granita

6 SERVINGS   64 CALORIES PER SERVING

¼ cup sugar
¼ cup water
2 cups chilled freshly squeezed pink grapefruit juice

1 tablespoon gold tequila (optional)
Pink grapefruit wedges, for garnish

1. Combine the sugar and water in a small saucepan. Bring to a boil, swirling the pan until the sugar is dissolved. Let the syrup cool to room temperature.

2. Pour the grapefruit juice into a medium bowl. Stir in the sugar syrup and the tequila. Pour into a 13 × 9-inch baking dish and place in a level spot in the freezer. Let stand until it begins to freeze, about 2 hours. Stir up the crystals and return to the freezer. Repeat, stirring two or three times, until the granita is completely frozen.

3. To serve, scrape the granita with a fork into chilled serving bowls. Garnish with grapefruit wedges.

Espresso-Orange Granita

6 SERVINGS   48 CALORIES PER SERVING

¼ cup sugar
¾ cup water
Grated zest of 1 small orange
1½ cups brewed espresso (regular or decaffeinated)
2 tablespoons Kahlua or other coffee liqueur

1. Combine the sugar and ¼ cup of the water in a small saucepan. Bring to a boil, swirling the pan until the sugar is dissolved. Add the orange zest and let cool to room temperature.

2. Strain the sugar syrup into a bowl and stir in the espresso, the Kahlua and the remaining ½ cup water. Pour into a 9 × 13-inch baking dish and place in a level spot in the freezer. Let stand until it begins to freeze, about 2 hours. Stir up the crystals and return to the freezer. Repeat, stirring two or three times, until the granita is completely frozen.

3. To serve, scrape the granita with a fork into chilled dessert bowls.

Sopaipillas

Even though these little "pillows" are fried, the dough absorbs a minuscule amount of the oil. This type of dessert or sweet snack is very typical in Mexico.

8 SERVINGS   200 CALORIES PER SERVING

3 tablespoons confectioners' sugar
2 teaspoons ground cinnamon
2 cups unbleached all-purpose flour
2 teaspoons baking powder
½ teaspoon salt
1 tablespoon unsalted butter
¾ cup flavorless vegetable oil

1. In a small bowl, mix together the confectioners' sugar and the cinnamon. Set aside.

2. Add the flour, baking powder and salt to a food processor and pulse several times to mix. Add the butter and process until the mixture is the consistency of coarse meal. With the machine, slowly pour in ½ cup of water and process until the dough just comes together; do not overmix. You may need to add 1 to 2 tablespoons more water if the mixture seems too dry.

3. Remove the dough from the processor and knead on a lightly floured surface for 5 minutes. Form the dough into a ball, cover with plastic wrap and let rest for 30 minutes.

4. Divide the dough into 8 equal portions (2 ounces each). Roll out each piece of dough into a round about ⅛ inch thick. Cut each round into 4 triangular quarters and set the pieces aside.

5. Heat the vegetable oil in a large skillet over medium-high heat. Place 4 to 6 pieces of the dough in the hot oil and fry the first side until pale golden, about 1 to 2 minutes. The dough will start to puff after several seconds. Turn the pieces and fry until golden. If the sopaipillas start to brown too quickly, reduce the heat. Drain well on paper towels, sprinkle the cinnamon sugar over the hot sopaipillas and serve at once.

Sangria

6 SERVINGS   143 CALORIES PER SERVING

½ cup fresh orange juice
¼ cup fresh lime juice
¼ to ⅓ cup sugar, to taste
3 cups of inexpensive, fruity dry red wine, such as Beaujolais or
    Zinfandel
1 cup chilled seltzer
1 lime, cut into thin slices
½ small navel orange, cut into thin slices

1. In a pitcher, combine the orange juice and lime juice. Add ¼ cup of the sugar and the wine and stir to dissolve the sugar. Cover and refrigerate until serving time.

2. Just before serving, add the seltzer and float the slices of lime and orange on the surface of the sangria.

Lemon-Lime Cooler

When you zest the citrus fruits, use a nutmeg grater or the fine side of a four-sided grater and grate only the colored outer layer; the white pith is bitter.

6 SERVINGS   79 CALORIES PER SERVING

Zest and juice of 5 small lemons
Zest and juice of 5 limes
½ cup sugar
4 cups ice water
2 cups chilled seltzer
Ice cubes

In a small pitcher, combine the lemon zest and juice, the lime zest and juice and the sugar. Stir with a long-handled spoon to dissolve the sugar. Just before serving, add the ice water and the seltzer. Serve in tall glasses over plenty of ice cubes.

Citrus Iced Tea

6 SERVINGS   48 CALORIES PER SERVING

6 cups water
6 tea bags
3 sprigs of fresh mint or 1 tablespoon dried
Zest and juice of 1 lemon
Zest and juice of 1 small orange
¼ cup sugar
1 lime, cut into 6 slices

1. In a medium saucepan, bring the water to a boil. Add the tea bags, mint, lemon zest, orange zest and sugar. Remove from the heat and let steep for 5 minutes.

2. Strain the tea through a fine sieve or a strainer lined with several layers of damp cheesecloth into a pitcher. Let cool slightly.

3. Stir in the lemon juice and orange juice. Cover and refrigerate until well chilled, about 2 hours. Serve in tall glasses, each garnished with a slice of lime.

Cantaloupe Cooler

6 SERVINGS   84 CALORIES PER SERVING

2 small very ripe cantaloupes
2 to 3 tablespoons sugar
Juice of 2 limes
3 cups ice water
3 cups seltzer

1. Quarter the melons and discard the seeds. Cut the peel off the melon and cut the melon into 1-inch cubes. Put the fruit into a food processor and pulse until coarsely puréed. Add the sugar and the lime juice and pulse several more times.

2. Pour the cantaloupe purée into a pitcher. Stir in the ice water and seltzer and serve immediately.

Rice Cooler

6 SERVINGS   137 CALORIES PER SERVING

> *1 cup white rice*
> *½ teaspoon ground cinnamon*
> *2 cups hot water*
> *3 tablespoons sugar*

1. Grind the rice in a spice grinder or blender to a fairly fine powder. Transfer to a heatproof jar, add the cinnamon and hot water and let stand until cool. Then cover and stand at room temperature overnight.

2. Pour the rice mixture into a blender or food processor and blend 3 minutes. Pour into a pitcher or medium bowl and stir in 2 cups of cold water. Whisk to blend well, then strain through a sieve lined with several layers of damp cheesecloth. Gather the edges of the cheesecloth together and twist to wring out as much liquid as possible.

3. Add 2 more cups of cold water. Stir in the sugar until dissolved. Cover and refrigerate until well chilled, at least 2 hours. Serve ice cold.

Banana-Pineapple Cooler

6 SERVINGS   128 CALORIES PER SERVING

> *3 cups canned pineapple juice*
> *2 ripe bananas, peeled and cut into 1-inch chunks*
> *1 can (8 ounces) pineapple chunks in unsweetened pineapple juice*
> *1 to 1½ cups chilled seltzer*
> *Ice cubes*

1. In a blender or food processor, combine 1½ cups of the pineapple juice, the bananas and the pineapple chunks with their juice. Purée until smooth.

2. Pour the purée into a pitcher. Add the remaining pineapple juice and enough seltzer to make 6 cups. Serve in tall glasses over ice.

Dried Hibiscus Flower Cooler

Dried hibiscus flowers, which have a tart, almost lemony flavor, provide the red coloring of many of the herbal teas on the market today. The dried flowers can be found at health food and herb stores.

6 SERVINGS   45 CALORIES PER SERVING

6 cups water
2 cups dried hibiscus flowers
¼ cup honey
Juice of 1 lime, or more to taste

In a small saucepan, bring the water to a boil. Add the hibiscus flowers, remove from the heat and let steep 10 minutes. Stir in the honey until dissolved and let steep 20 minutes longer. Strain the liquid into a small pitcher and add lime juice to taste. Cover and refrigerate until chilled, about 2 hours, before serving.

Creamy Fruit Cooler

For this refreshing and nutritious drink, popular in many warm Latin American countries, choose the ripest, most aromatic fruit you can find.

1 SERVING   149 CALORIES PER SERVING

1 cup ice cold skim milk
¼ of a ripe banana
2 large strawberries, sliced
¼ of a medium ripe mango, peeled

Place all the ingredients in a blender or food processor and purée until smooth. Serve at once.

Mexican Coffee

6 Servings   45 Calories per serving

8 cups water
¼ cup dark brown sugar
3 cinnamon sticks
1½ cups freshly ground medium-grind coffee

Bring the water to a boil in a medium nonaluminum saucepan. Add the brown sugar and cinnamon sticks and simmer 15 minutes. Whisk in the coffee grounds and return to a boil. Remove the pan from the heat, cover and let steep about 5 minutes. Strain the hot coffee through a sieve lined with several layers of damp cheesecloth. Serve at once.

Spiced Coffee

A cup of spiced coffee is the perfect way to end a Mexican meal or any other festive occasion.

6 Servings   7 Calories per serving

6 cups strong, freshly brewed coffee
1 cinnamon stick, crushed
3 to 4 whole cloves
½ teaspoon anise seeds
Zest from 1 small orange, peeled from the orange with a vegetable peeler
3 tablespoons dark brown sugar (optional)

Combine all the ingredients in a medium saucepan and warm over very low heat 30 minutes. Do not let the coffee boil. Strain and serve.

Coffee Gelatin with Kahlua

If you can afford the extra 27 calories per tablespoon, top this light dessert with a dollop of unsweetened whipped cream flavored with vanilla.

6 SERVINGS   61 CALORIES PER SERVING

> *1 tablespoon unflavored gelatin*
> *2 tablespoons sugar*
> *2 tablespoons instant espresso coffee*
> *⅓ cup Kahlua or other coffee liqueur*

1. Soften the gelatin in 2 cups of cold water.

2. In a small saucepan, heat ⅔ cup of water with the sugar and instant espresso over medium-low heat, stirring until the sugar is dissolved. Stir in the softened gelatin and Kahlua and stir until the gelatin dissolves.

3. Divide the liquid among 6 half-cup dessert glasses and refrigerate until set, about 2 hours.

INDEX